TO THE
BEACH

TO THE BEACH

THOR KERR

U W
A P
SCHOLARLY

First published in 2015 by
UWA Publishing
Crawley, Western Australia 6009
www.uwap.uwa.edu.au

THE UNIVERSITY OF
WESTERN
AUSTRALIA

A full CIP data entry is available from the National Library of Australia.

Printed by Lightning Source

CONTENTS

ACKNOWLEDGEMENTS

This book was written with the support of a Curtin University postdoctoral fellowship in the School of Media, Culture and Creative Arts. The school provided the time and place for me to write this book in the company of some of Western Australia's great contemporary writers and scholars. Interaction with colleagues and students in the school over the course of this fellowship has been an important source of inspiration and feedback for this book.

To the Beach would not have been written without the steadfast support of Steve Mickler, who supervised my PhD thesis at Curtin University from which this book was created. Inspiration for its creation also came from Vijay Devadas at University of Otago, who pointed out improvements in the thesis and encouraged me to communicate its research findings to a more general audience. I must also thank Shaphan Cox from Curtin's Department of Geography, who has supported the project through our many conversations about Fremantle's culture, politics and planning. Gordon and the team at the Veggie Patch provided the coffee and cheer behind this book while Yiyik and David Kerr performed admirably as its early readers.

In writing this book, I have relied heavily on the public engagement of the people named in it, and the openness of some to discussing their public contributions. In gaining permission to reproduce images in this book, I must thank Adele Carles,

Rowena Skinner of the Greens and Steve Grant of the *Fremantle Herald*. Cartoons from the *Fremantle Herald* and *The West Australian* newspapers have been reproduced here in place of publicity images for North Port Quay, for which reproduction permission was not granted. However, I am grateful to Peter Newman for directing me to North Port Quay's project manager, Chris Carman, who made a representation on my behalf regarding those images. I must also thank members of my family for the use of their photographs and art.

Gratitude is owed to Christina Lee for advice on writing the book proposal, and to Terri-ann White for recognising its potential and guiding this manuscript through to publication. I must also thank Kate Pickard for handling the paperwork and Anna Maley-Fadgyas, Mike Kuszla and J&M Typesetting for polishing the manuscript and arranging its production.

Thor Kerr
January, 2015

FOR PLEASURE

Photograph by Prapti Widinugraheni

Port Beach begins where the stone-locked, reclaimed land at Rous Head comes ashore. This broad white beach stretches a mile north until it is known as Leighton Beach, veering east then continuing north to the rocks before Perth's hip Cottesloe Beach.

Port Beach is a place for sunbathing, swimming, dog walking and whatever between the big blue of the Indian Ocean and the colourful stacks of shipping containers lining Fremantle's Inner Harbour. Port Beach is not paradise fit for a Bounty Bar, but locals' desire for it sank a multi-billion-dollar property development and helped turn Labor's political heartland into the Greens' City of Fremantle. The thought of developers threatening this beach helped Greens members win local lower-house and upper-house seats in Western Australia's parliament, as well as the mayoral seat and other council positions. The Greens' wave that swept through Fremantle in 2009 built its momentum on the public reaction to the idea of a walled city threatening the beach and its community. This walled city was envisaged to withstand the rising waves of climate change, but it could not withstand the rising waves of public antagonism that eventually drowned it. North Port Quay was created for a global apocalyptic future, not the local democratic present. Supporting it was a big mistake.

'It was a perfect location because the area was degraded',[2] claimed Greg Poland, who inspired and headed the consortium behind North Port Quay. Poland planned to make a big investment in the project through his Strzelecki Group, which had developed large marina properties on Perth's metropolitan coast to the north and the south of Fremantle. The man was used to getting his way; although, occasionally, local publics got in the way of him. He needed a good reason for reclaiming land in the waters off Port Beach, and Poland thought he had found it. 'When you get older you start to change your opinion and you start to get smarter and you get more educated,' he said. 'When we started doing this project I wanted it to be environmentally friendly and carbon free.' Not sure how to go about it, Poland 'brought on some good expertise and told them: my instructions are it's got to be right, it's got to be good'. [3]

Topped with oiled-back, silver hair, Poland was a formidable presence: the hyper-real image of a 1980s property developer. Within a dark jacket, Poland kept his shirt wide open for business. No tie, no jewellery, just authentic chest hair. Poland positioned himself as a champion of Western Australians. Perhaps he believed he really was. In Australian drawl, he emphasised words like 'the people' in an accent closer to that of former Labor leader Bob Hawke than any man of such substantial capital. Yet Poland knew what drove him to create North Port Quay: 'this is not a building that's going to be pulled down in 50 years. This is going to be around for decades, generations, hundreds of years, thousands of years hopefully.' This would be Poland's legacy: 'I don't want my children, definitely don't want my grandchildren, great grandchildren to look at me and say "he was a vandal". I want them to say "he was visionary".' Poland wanted to leave his mark – a heritage legacy for 'the people of Western Australia'. As part of this new-found wisdom, he pledged not to 'do anything wrong environmentally' under any circumstances: 'I don't think you can afford to do it emotionally, financially and historically. You have got to do the right thing, especially when it comes to your family.'[4] But other people had other views, particularly about property development at the beach.

In the heart of Fremantle there are no longer any beaches, save the minor concave of Bathers Beach below the Round House fort, the first building of the Swan River colony. The beaches that once existed here have been converted through reclamation into parks and boat harbours so that sand is not encountered again until South Beach, at the southern end of the Fremantle Sailing Club. Unlike Port and Leighton beaches, which are exposed to the wind and waves of the Indian Ocean, South Beach is protected by Cockburn Sound. South Beach is tame and family functional: calm waters by a narrow beach, small dunes before grassed picnic areas containing a playground, barbeques, changing facilities and a decent cafe. The beaches around Fremantle evoke popular appeal because they mean different things to different people.[5] Everyone can have a unique day at the beach. Diverse people with diverse experiences share the fact that these days may be remembered, and this memory collection can be used for imagining community.[6] Urban beaches, although transformed by forgotten human action, form an important symbolic connection between an ideal of unadulterated nature and a collective ideal of Australia.[7] Fremantle's beaches provide relief from the everyday pressures of urban life. On the beach, obligations diminish against an ocean horizon, against the smells and sounds of sea meeting shore. The beach is a place for seeing other possibilities; a place for recognising the imposition of common sense and resisting it.[8] The beach seems natural to us because it appears outside human regulation, outside the realm of human property and beyond hegemony of commoditisation. Exposure to physical sensations of the beach, this experience of pleasure, opens up the way we think about ourselves. It helps loosen the binding conventions we have learned and adopted to govern ourselves.[9] Both this pleasure of freedom and the continually changing forms of beaches contribute to them remaining commons rather than the property of individuals. The sense of beaches being beyond human regulation, being too dynamic for property surveying, makes it difficult to commoditise and trade them. Constructing borders within beaches is hugely problematic, but using beaches as symbolic borders around a community can appear natural.

News of North Port Quay broke in *The West Australian* newspaper on the morning of the project's official launch on Thursday,
29 May 2008. An image of the project occupied almost half of
the front page of the state's only daily newspaper. A reader looked
down on the interior of North Port Quay – an empty, hyper-
modern city featuring a wide central canal surrounded by a vast,
orderly assortment of low- and high-rise buildings. The only signs
of life appeared to be constrained within two, or perhaps three,
boats travelling up the canal. North Port Quay was a mechanical,
futuristic city without people. Its flat landscape divided into erect,
autonomous blocks by well-defined, untravelled roads. 'The $10b
plan for Freo island' seemed more like a circuit board than part
of the City of Fremantle, known for its late-nineteenth-century
retro streetscape. The signification of North Port Quay as a hyper-
modern city, alien to Fremantle, was not lost on newspaper staff,
who described it as 'a grand Dubai development, only this one's
proposed for the Fremantle coast'. The newspaper announced that
Fremantle's long-standing member of parliament Jim McGinty
didn't like it. Instead of a public-relations coup, North Port Quay's
occupation of *The West Australian*'s front page suggested a looming
transgression in Fremantle. However, editorial and imagery
inside,[10] on page 3, seemed to favour the project's fruition:

> North Port Quay will sit north of Fremantle behind a
> 3.5km seawall designed to withstand global warming
> and storm surges and include homes for 20,000 people,
> 100,000sqm of office space, Venice-style canals and
> bridges, two new schools, 2200 boat pens, a performing-
> arts centre, a five-star hotel and convention centre.

North Port Quay was described from its proponents' perspectives without any overtly dissenting voices. The project director, Chris Carman, was given three paragraphs, sustainability expert Professor Peter Newman was 'enlisted' to support the project for four paragraphs, North Port Quay spokesman Mike Holtham was given two paragraphs and the project's master planner, Mike Day, had three paragraphs. Images supporting this page-3 article seemed less alien than the front-cover rendering. They showed people on a distant canal beach and North Port Quay fitting snugly alongside Fremantle's port. Readers were also informed that the project would 'face significant hurdles', which Chris Carmen hoped to overcome by selling the idea to Fremantle community through months of public consultation: '10,000 promotional DVDs and pamphlets' would be sent 'to every residential address in Fremantle' to promote this 'carbon emission–free development' and its 'Fremantle-friendly sweeteners'. These sweeteners included boat pens, new beaches, a surf reef, a seawall for use as a fishing platform, renewable-energy production and rehabilitation of the seabed damaged by port activities.

The West Australian's coverage continued with an internet version of the article accompanied by a blog and poll headed: 'A shrewd plan to tackle the city's booming population woes or an environmental nightmare?' Readers were asked to see North Port Quay as a new technology to cope with Perth's rising population or an environmental nightmare that would damage Fremantle. The poll result suggested that 70 per cent of an undisclosed number of respondents considered North Port Quay a coping technology and 30 per cent considered it a nightmare. The blog attracted 134 responses – 99 on the project's launch day. The blog comments were less supportive than the poll. Many derided North Port Quay for being a playground for wealthy elites doomed by the environmental blowback of consumerism. Parody was directed at the project, 'Smithers Says':

> I say build it! As global warming takes its grip and a huge winter frontal system or remnants of a tropical cyclone drift down the coast, combined with a king tide and rising sea level – I'll be keen to see what happens. During an event like this I can't wait to see all of those precious mega-rich Perth tossers running out of their newly rendered McMansions, all of those born-to-rule small-business proprietors and, of course, WA's local CUBs all running to their European cars and Toorak tractors trying to get out as the entire edifice gets hammered by a storm created by rampant Western consumerism. Bring it on.

'SickofPessimism' responded in all seriousness that seawall building experts would be capable of solving any rising seas threatening North Port Quay. Other comments favouring the project argued that an earlier Mandurah canal development had not ended in environmental crisis as predicted and that it was a model for other coastal developments around Perth. North Port Quay would be a sustainable development preventing urban sprawl, a model for other cities. It would help Perth to do better in a presumed global competition of post-industrial cities associated with sustainable development. 'Jude' argued:

> It seems like a brilliant opportunity for the WA government to prove it's not all about exploiting the country for resources as the development looks like it can set a global benchmark in sustainable development – something

which developers around the world can learn from.

Jude argued North Port Quay deserved a fair go: 'it would be environmentally criminal not to consider it' as a solution to the problems he articulated. These included a metropolitan land shortage due to native-title claims, environmental destruction through suburban development and the lack of an 'international benchmark for high-quality carbon-free developments'. As the online argument shifted to carbon emissions, North Port Quay was challenged for ignoring 'the many thousands of tonnes of diesel required to move that amount of earth' and for needlessly threatening a marine environment when there was surplus land for development around Perth.

By the evening of 29 May, North Port Quay's launch had been covered in news broadcasts for the Perth Metropolitan area by all major television stations.[11] These news broadcasts focused on the launch using video footage of the project's 3D model and associated information supplied by the North Port Quay consortium. They also included footage of the launch press conference and interviews with opponents. Major news themes included the ambitious scale of the project over the sea, its sustainability credentials and the immediate controversy surrounding it. Public broadcaster the ABC[12] constructed public controversy around North Port Quay as a rationale for introducing this marketing initiative to viewers:

> ANCHOR: A controversial plan to build a $6 billion man-made island village off the coast of Fremantle is already drawing fierce opposition. Leading the criticism is the Premier Mr Alan Carpenter, who says the plan makes no sense and that he hopes it never happens.

VLS High Angle. A digital 3D model of North Port Quay emerges as an island out of the sea: starting as a plan, then becoming grey concrete forms with zoom in. Subtitle: 'Corporate video'.

Voiceover: It is known as North Point Quay…

LS High Angle. Camera pans left as the grey concrete forms become a coloured built environment, a modern city of low- and high-rise buildings amid orderly streets and blue canals with the ocean and a blurred shoreline in background.

Voiceover: and it is being sold as an environmentally friendly development like nothing ever seen in Australia.

CS Chris Carmen in front of a blind-covered window and blue screen bearing project images and the text 'Mandurah Ocean Marina Entered by Benchmark Projects'. Subtitle: 'Chris Carman NORTH PORT QUAY'.

Chris Carman: We truly believe that this is going to be a world-class model of sustainable development.

Voiceover: The development would be powered with renewable energy…

VLS High Angle. Model of urban islands behind seawall. Camera pans left.

Voiceover: but with cars allowed on the islands the proponents were forced to qualify their claim…

MS High Angle. Model of seawall, with cars on it, a canal in middle ground and buildings, roads and trees in background. Camera pans right along seawall with cars travelling upon it.

11

VOICEOVER: that it would be one of the world's first carbon-free developments.

CS. Peter Newman sitting in the same place as Chris Carmen was earlier. Subtitle: 'Peter Newman NORTH PORT QUAY'.

PETER NEWMAN: It's going to be carbon-free in terms of the way in which the people who are living there are powered.

LS High Angle. Model of a large low-rise structure, with several medium-rise buildings, a canal then the seawall, ocean and the coast behind it, a canal and several low-rise buildings on left. Camera pans left then cuts to a model of a large glass building in middle ground and Fremantle Port in background. Then a grand canal with several bridges over it leading to more buildings.

VOICEOVER: The project has the financial backing of forty of the state's most influential business people and property developers.

VLS High Angle. The port facility in middle ground, the Swan River mouth and Fremantle in background and sea in foreground, right and background. Camera pans right from the port out to sea.

VOICEOVER: But the premier says it would cause horrendous problems for the area.

ALAN CARPENTER: I don't like it.

CS. Alan Carpenter with tree and brick building in the background. Subtitle: 'Alan Carpenter PREMIER'.

ALAN CARPENTER: I won't support it, I oppose it, and it doesn't make any sense to me whatsoever and as long as I am able to I will oppose it.

MS. Port Beach with Colin Barnett [future premier and standing Member of Parliament for Cottesloe] talking to reporter in foreground with the port facility and sea in background.

VOICEOVER: The local MP has accused the developers of arrogance...

CS. Back of Colin Barnett, facing reporter with an otherwise empty beach and uninterrupted ocean horizon in background.

VOICEOVER: for eyeing off an area owned by the state.

CS. Colin Barnet speaking with beach and the Fremantle Port's seawall in background. Subtitle: 'Colin Barnett COTTESLOE MP'.

COLIN BARNETT: I am totally opposed to reclaiming seabed for housing.

The report then cut to alfresco seating at Gino's cafe in Fremantle's popular South Terrace, then to a shot of the mayor, Peter Tagliaferri, appearing undecided: 'It is a big development but I think it's a conversation that we shouldn't just shut out'. The next shot was of an eroded sand dune with a seawall in the background, followed by one of ocean scientist Chari Pattiarachi of the University of Western Australia warning that the project would cause long-term erosion problems for nearby beaches. The news returned to North Port Quay's simulation, focusing on the extent of its seawall as the voiceover said the project would be protected from storm surges and rising sea levels. Peter

Newman assured that the project's inhabitants would be better off than people living in a suburb further up the Swan River. Finally, the reporter stood at Rous Head – sea and beach in the background – to say that despite growing opposition, the developers would seek environmental, leasing, planning and development approvals.

The beach was a major visual element in news reporting of opposition to North Port Quay. The media constructed the idea of 'growing opposition' as a response to the seabed being occupied by wealthy developers and nearby public beaches being eroded. The project was also problematised by television visuals cutting back and forth between simulated flights over a futuristic canal city and footage of coastal waters by Fremantle Port, footage of a beach and footage of an ocean horizon. The simulated images of the project from plan to sprouting grey blocks, rendered colourful, captured the attention of journalists, who compared it to current images of Fremantle coast while constructing controversy around North Port Quay.

The project simulations were made available on North Port Quay's website. Its homepage showed a video of the development magically transforming itself over water from plan, to concrete blocks, then to a colourful, futuristic island city. The simulation was accompanied by soothing background music and a voiceover introducing the development in terms of its coastal metropolitan location and its leadership in ecological modernisation:

> Voiceover: Nestled between the Indian Ocean and Perth, North Port Quay will set a new standard in environmentally sustainable development. North Port Quay will set the standard by which all other developments will be judged. Homes and businesses will be powered

by wind, wave and solar energy. It will be a carbon-free development that actually creates a better environment.

During the video, background slides on the homepage changed so that a grand canal in the animated foreground corresponded to a photograph of leisure boats at harbour in the background, and a simulated aerial perspective of a beach at North Port Quay corresponded with a background picture of a lone surfer catching a wave. Photographs of past coastal leisure were combined with simulations of an urban coastal future. The voiceover described this as 'a place for people, with homes, schools, cafes, beaches, fishing platforms, cycle paths and walkways'. However, rather than showing happy people cycling, walking or fishing, the simulation showed cars travelling along bridges and the long seawall surrounding North Port Quay. This inconsistency was sensed by media workers covering the launch and it would repeatedly disrupt the consortium's 'carbon-free development' claim.

Articles on North Port Quay were published in Australia's main daily newspapers,[13] but national coverage subsided quickly, as did the internet chatter around posted images and information about the project.[14] North Port Quay was an important issue for Western Australian media audiences for several weeks, but it would remain a big issue for at least another year in Fremantle's press, and become a catalyst for the radical transformation of the area's electoral representation.

Notes

1   'WA Premier criticises Fremantle island plan', ABC News WA, Perth, 29 May 2008.

2   *Why are you focusing on environmental sustainability?*, North Port Quay, Perth, viewed 9 June 2011, <http://www.northportquay.com.au/Home/the-vision.html>.

3   Ibid.

4   Ibid.

5   J. Fiske, B. Hodge & G. Turner, *Myths of Oz: Reading Australian Popular Culture,* Allen & Unwin, North Sydney, 1987, p. 72.

6   B. Anderson, *Imagined Communities: Reflections on the Origin and Spread of Nationalism,* Verso, London, 1991.

7   Fiske, Hodge & Turner, *Myths of Oz*, pp. 54–5.

8   *The West Australian*, 22 September 2010, p. 1.

9   Fiske, Hodge & Turner, *Myths of Oz*, pp. 70–71.

10 *The West Australian*, 29 May 2008, p. 1.

11 T. Kerr, 'Representing ecological threats and negotiating green built environments', PhD thesis, Curtin University, 2012.

12 'WA Premier criticises Fremantle island plan', ABC News WA, Perth, 29 May 2008.

13 *The Australian Financial Review*, 30 May 2008, p. 1; *The Australian*, 30 May 2008, p. 2.

14 T. Kerr, 'Representing ecological threats and negotiating green built environments', PhD thesis, Curtin University, 2012.

COLONISATION

Photograph by Indi Kerr

'We're trying to practise the kind of community building our forebears practised in the 1800s. Generations of people will live, work, play and be educated in these new urban settlements.'[1]
North Port Quay's master planner, Mike Day

Sustainable development has become an important concern in Fremantle and it can be appropriated readily for property development. Appropriation of public concern has been integral to the discourse around colonial land occupation in the area since as far back as the late 1820s. Naval officer James Stirling used the British press to spin doctor concern about the threat of French competition to gain support in London for his plan to settle the coastal area in and around the towns he named 'Fremantle' on the mouth of the Swan River, and 'Perth' further upstream.[2] The eviction of local Aboriginal people began through a discourse involving maps, property surveys, and language that justified vicious acts of exclusion. Stirling named the northern headland of the Swan River 'Rous Head' and the southern headland 'Arthur's Head' after fellow colonial officers.[3] This eviction process continues through general exclusion of Nyoongar words on European-imagined maps of the area,[4] through criminalising images, disproportionate imprisonment, and non-recognition of Aboriginal sovereignty.[5]

The coastal plain around Fremantle and Perth was swiftly surveyed, occupied and enclosed by Stirling's settlers – backed by the force of British arms and symbols of entitlement – excluding the Nyoongar people who lived and worked there.[6] Entitlement to land under the colonial institution depended on a white fellow demonstrating his capital for improving the site's economic value.[7] These men and favoured colonial officers were awarded initial occupation rights by Stirling on behalf of the British Crown. To convert these occupation rights into land title, grant holders or their agents had to show improvement in the capital of land within ten years or their occupation rights would revert to the British Crown for reissue to alternative white men with capital. Land grants were sold by some grantees as early as 1831, and by 1832 the land-grant system had been replaced by the selling of Crown land.[8] The British invaders, as they were referred to by Stirling, ignored the land–occupation regulation and spatial organisation of the invaded Nyoongar people, who suffered exclusion from their land by foreigners.[9] Nyoongar resistance to this social, economic and cultural disruption was met by overwhelming violence from British capitalists, their servants, troops, muskets and horses. The Colonial Office regarded the Swan River settlement as a private-land speculation by capitalists,[10] but provided sufficient funds and military support for it to endure. In his settlement proclamation, Stirling asserted that he could grant occupation rights to all 'unoccupied land' in the area. However, this wording was replaced by the term 'wasteland' in settlement regulations because the land was too obviously already occupied.[11] Enclosing and seizing 'wastelands' belonging to Nyoongar people was partly legitimised for settlers by the pre-existing practice of enclosing and privatising common lands and wastelands in the United Kingdom through enclosure acts. The Colonial Office did not constrain Stirling's allocation of Nyoongar country to the invading settlers, but it was fastidious about how much water frontage was granted to any one of them. The settlement's 1829 regulations allocated land grants with a maximum 25 per cent perimeter as river frontage.[12] Land title was withheld to ocean-frontage land at Arthur's Head – which Stirling had claimed for himself – in anticipation of the land being required for the 'security, health or general convenience of the Public at large'.[13] In supporting Stirling's claim to ocean-front land at Arthur's head, the main shareholder of the Fremantle Whaling Company wrote that any reallocation of Stirling's land with all the company's 'improvements upon it…would tend to destroy all confidence in colonial property, and put an end to Colonial Enterprise'.[14] The historical record shows that claims for public convenience have rubbed up against claims for capitalist enterprise since the earliest British discussion of coastal-land enti-tlement around Fremantle. These claims and counterclaims about colonial categorisations of land have reinforced colonial control by drowning out Nyoongar voices on the social organisation of this space.

Considerable resources have been dedicated towards the defence of Fremantle port – militarily and culturally – since Captain Fremantle's arrival by boat almost two centuries ago. Fremantle has an art museum, a military museum, a shipwreck museum and a vast maritime museum. The shipwreck museum provides an overview of European, particularly Dutch, contributions to voyages of discovery and trade with the Far East. It features salvaged imperial wealth, including the portico gateway to the Dutch colonial port fortress in Batavia (now Jakarta). The maritime museum includes a display of Australia's failed defence of the America's Cup in yacht races off Fremantle port. The display reproduces media records of Australia challenging the power of the USA by winning the cup in 1983. This was a symbolic event of imperial proportion given that the Americans had won the British cup from under the nose of Queen Victoria in 1851, and then kept it. However, Australia's challenge to US power proved short-lived, and the cup was returned to America after defeat in Fremantle in 1987. Besides featuring the America's Cup, this large museum has displays dedicated to European arrivals and the foundation of the Western Australia colony, maritime technologies, and local contributions to major wars since Australian Federation. This naturalisation of Australia is disrupted by a single Indonesian *prau* – the kind of wooden boat seized and destroyed by coastguards defending Australian waters. A display panel chronicles 'Setting up the Borders': in 1829 Britain claimed 3-mile territorial waters around Western Australia; in 1953 Australia was the first nation to claim the resources of an entire continental shelf; in 1968 Australia's territorial waters were increased to 12 nautical miles; and in 1979 its territorial waters were extended to 200 nautical miles from the coast. This display suggests that the Indian Ocean aggressor is Australia rather than the impoverished Indonesian fishermen captured by the Australian defence force. It works to disrupt belief in Australia's borders being natural and fixed far back in time. There is no natural Australian border, only an imagined one. The beach seems like a natural border to Australians. The beach is the original invasion scene, the place of exclusion, of racial division, of endless vigilance and of fear.[15] It is also centre stage for performing Australian life. In December 2005, this performance turned violent at Cronulla Beach when thousands of white Australians formed a mob to attack racially identified 'non-Australians':

> One participant likens the day's events to facing the (mythical) possibility of Japanese invasion in the Second World War. For others it stands for Anzac Day, for a memorial picnic at Gallipoli, for the turning away of the *Tampa*, for the streets of Iraq. It is homeland.[16]

Beaches support both the performance of territoriality and the stimulation of pleasure. It is, therefore, not surprising that more people gather to defend Perth's metropolitan beaches against property development than to save other apparently natural environments from developer incursion. In the Fremantle coastal area there have been several major confrontations between property developers and local activists. The Save Freo Beaches Alliance rallied against the Three Harbours Policy to enclose the ocean from Bathers' Beach to South Beach within an arc of hotels, apartments and boating facilities. Locals were called upon to defend the coast:

> Australian beaches are PUBLIC beaches. If YOU are against the proposed changes to YOUR beaches then YOU must act NOW... [17]

On 20 January 2008, 2,500 people attended the alliance's awareness and fundraising event by the beach. Some carried signs:

'WE SHALL FIGHT THEM ON THE BEACHES'.[18] Musician John Butler entertained the 'enthusiastic crowd of beach lovers'.[19]

Some property developers have tried to head off coastal-activist challenges by publicising their project's green credentials. Stockland presented its Fremantle South Beach development as a sustainability initiative: 'South Beach represents best practice in environmentally sustainable design; including water management in the public realm, waterwise plant selection and passive solar design'.[20] Locals opposed to Stockland's development argued that its construction would disturb old industrial ground and cause toxic contamination. They also argued against the project's privatisation of public coastline and its destruction of the South Beach foreshore.[21] But Stockland's blocks of luxury apartments were built and sold. Developers were attempting to produce a clean, green self-image, and they had some successes. But their attempt to market projects as 'green' came at a time of increasing public awareness of unethical practices by property developers seeking governmental approval for coastal projects. The issue became glaringly obvious after Western Australia's Corruption and Crime Commission began investigating allegations of council manipulation by developers of large coastal properties in the Southwest of Western Australia. In 2005, the commission investigated attempts by representatives of the Canal Rocks property project at Smiths Beach 'to influence the Busselton Shire Council, public officers and politicians to support the development'.[22] These investigations tracked the activities of lobbyists Brian Burke and Julian Grill from the Smiths Beach project through to their involvement in a Port Coogee development on a site of former industrial land, beach and seabed just south of Fremantle.[23] Public hearings were held into the Smiths Beach development in 2006, and the Port Coogee development in 2007. The Port Coogee hearing publicised large cash donations made by the project's proponents to the successful re-election campaign of then Cockburn mayor, Stephen Lee. Through these public hearings and their media coverage, the community of Fremantle and Western Australia learned much about the alleged wrongdoings of coastal property developers. They also saw how the developers' consultants and lobbyists could affect the outcomes of municipal elections, and the partiality of public officials. Although Burke, Grill, Lee and others were not prosecuted in relation to these investigations, by 2008 Western Australian media audiences were well aware of transgression in the privatisation of coastal land. This awareness increased the legitimacy and popularity of people and organisations resisting property development on the beaches around Fremantle.

It was into this context that North Port Quay was launched by a consortium of more than thirty property developers and investors.[24] The consortium was led by Strzelecki Group,[25] which had been set up in the 1980s to undertake the Sorrento Quay development overlooking the Indian Ocean at Hillarys Boat Harbour, about 20 kilometres north of Fremantle. The group went on to develop Dolphin Quay and several other large waterfront property projects at the Mandurah Ocean Marina, 50 kilometres south of Fremantle. The North Port Quay consortium set out to represent Fremantle community's acceptance of the project in planning negotiations with the state government and Fremantle Ports. This local-legitimacy strategy became increasingly important after the project's goodwill credentials began collapsing within a week of its launch. Images of North Port Quay's principal lobbyist John Halden were repeatedly published in *The West Australian* alongside images of disgraced lobbyists Grill and Burke in relation to communications between lobbyists, politicians and public servants.[26] Focusing on community acceptance, project director

Chris Carman said it would take up to nine months of public consultation to sell the idea of North Port Quay to Fremantle.[27] The project's master planner, Mike Day, promised the project would emulate the urban fabric of Fremantle using modern design and practising 'the kind of community building our forebears practised in the 1800s. Generations of people will live, work, play and be educated in these new urban settlements'.[28] Day didn't recognise that these development practices had overwritten and evicted pre-existing culture and community. Day presumed that sufficient legitimacy for the project could be gained by reworking some elements of Fremantle such as 'a compact, connected, mixed use, walkable neighbourhood' and 'all the diverse housing types'.[29] Given the coastal-activist trouble other developers had faced in getting ocean-front developments off the ground around Fremantle, the consortium positioned North Port Quay as a greater good. It recruited the services of 'one of WA's leading environmentalists'[30] Professor Peter Newman as a spokesman and sustainability consultant for the project. Newman, an urban planner known locally for defending Fremantle's railway station against closure, headed the five-month-old Curtin University Sustainability Policy (CUSP) Institute which was promised scholarship funding by the consortium for its engagement in the project. Newman came out in favour of the project from the day of its launch:

> Professor Newman said he supported the proposal because it created a dense, compact, carbon emission–free development which used renewable energy and public transport and would create a better environment than the one it replaces. It created thousands of homes in the inner-metropolitan area, rather than contributing to suburban sprawl.[31]

The consortium's legitimisation strategy rested on a struggle for common-sense acceptance of North Port Quay as 'green'. This played out in Fremantle's local newspapers, political campaigns, candidate debates and council meetings. The consortium associated the project with sustainable development and argued that North Port Quay 'could become the world's first carbon-free development'.[32] Advertisements and articles about the project in Fremantle's local press clustered around the project's launch in May 2008, the state election in September 2008 and the Fremantle by-election in May 2009. However, the consortium's attempt to claim the environmental high ground, particularly during election campaigns, backfired spectacularly. The ecological benefits of the project in a carbon-constrained future articulated by North Port Quay's proponents were rebutted by the ecological risk of the project's construction; their representations about investing in the city's future were negated by counterclaims of unacceptable risk for the present Fremantle community. The threat of North Port Quay would become an effective discursive weapon, wielded most effectively by Adele Carles of the Greens party to win the Fremantle seat in Western Australia's parliament – an unprecedented electoral victory for the Greens that ended eighty-five years of continuous Labor party representation.

Notes

1   *The West Australian*, 29 May 2008, p. 1.

2   P. Statham-Drew, *James Stirling: Admiral and Founding Governor of Western Australia,* University of Western Australia Press, Crawley, 2003, pp. 110–40.

3   Statham-Drew, *James Stirling*, pp. 66–73.

4   S. Mickler, 'The battle for Goonininup', *Arena*, vol. 96, Spring, 1991, pp. 69–88.

5   T. Kerr & S. Cox, *Setting up the Nyoongar Tent Embassy: a Report on Perth Media*, Ctrl-Z Press, Perth, 2013.

6   Ibid., pp. 146–85.

7   Ibid., p. 120.

8   Ibid., p. 204.

9   B. Carter & L. Nutter, *Nyungah Land: Records of Invasion and Theft of Aboriginal Land on the Swan River 1829–1850*, Swan Valley Nyungah Community, Guildford, 2005, pp. 4–98; Statham-Drew, *James Stirling*, pp. 74–281.

10 Statham-Drew, *James Stirling*, p. 232.

11 Carter & Nutter, *Nyungah Land*, pp. 4–28.

12 Statham-Drew, *James Stirling*, p. 146.

13 Ibid., p. 424.

14 Ibid.

15 S. Perera, *Australia and the Insular Imagination: Beaches, Borders, Boats, and Bodies*, Palgrave Macmillan, New York, 2009.

16 Ibid., p. 150.

17 *Save Freo Beaches Alliance*, Save Freo Beaches Alliance, Perth, viewed 17 August 2010, <http://www.savefreobeaches.com/savefreobeaches.com/Home.html>.

18 *Crowd 2*, Save Freo Beaches Alliance, Perth, viewed 17 August 2010, <http://www.savefreobeaches.com/savefreobeaches.com/Gallery/Pages/save_freo_beaches_events_files.html#0>.

19 *Family Day Event*, Save Freo Beaches Alliance, Perth, viewed 17 August 2010, <http://www.savefreobeaches.com/savefreobeaches.com/Activities/Entries/2008/1/20_Family_Day_Event.html>.

20 *South Beach & Sustainability*, Stockland Corporation, Sydney, viewed 8 May 2009, <http://www.southbeachvillage.com.au/SouthBeachSustainability.cfm>.

21 I. Jamieson, *Rally to save Freo's South Beach*, Green Left Weekly, 22 October 2003, viewed 17 August 2010, <http://www.greenleft.org.au/node/28880>.

22 Corruption and Crime Commission, *Report on the Investigation of Alleged Misconduct Concerning Mr Stephen Lee, Mayor of the City of Cockburn*, Government of Western Australia, Perth, 2008, p. 1.

23 ibid., p. 29.

24 *The West Australian*, 29 May 2008, p. 1.

25 Strzelecki Group, *About Us,* Strzelecki Group, 2009, viewed 20 August 2010, <www.strzeleckigroup.com.au>.

26 *The West Australian*, 4 June 2008, p. 2; *The West Australian*, 5 June 2008, p. 21.

27 *The West Australian*, 29 May 2008, p. 3.

28 Ibid.

29 Ibid.

30 *Today Tonight*, 2008, North Port Quay, Perth, viewed 20 August 2010, <http://www.northportquay.com.au/Archive/tv-archive.html>.
31 *The West Australian*, 29 May 2008, p. 3.
32 *Fremantle Herald*, 14 June 2008, p. 7.

ARRIVAL

Representation of North Port Quay in *The West Australian*

'North Port Quay would create an entirely new, environmentally sustainable coastal location and could become the world's first carbon-free development.'[1]

North Port Quay

What do we know of sustainable development? We've arrived at this term through a coincidence of environmental and governmental-reform discourses, traceable at least as far back as Roman architect Vitruvius' speaking against lead poisoning caused by air pollution.[2] More recently, from the control centre of an invasive British Empire, Thomas Malthus demanded sexual regulation to avoid misery and extinction through rapid population growth.[3] His desire to limit other people's reproductive pleasure has been challenged by many, but his notion of Earth's limited carrying capacity has been reproduced without much criticism as a key feature of sustainable development.[4] In the early 1970s, Earth's finite capacity for absorbing pollution from and providing resources for global population and economic expansion became widely discussed concepts. *The Limits to Growth* report[5] stimulated public debate about the trajectory of society – with unchecked economic and population growth – leading to an uninhabitable planet. This paved the way for sustainable development to become the solution to Earth's limits, as articulated in a United Nations report calling for the regulation of technology and social relations (where Malthus had argued for control of sexual relations).[6] Sustainable development was accepted as a consensus-building solution enshrined in Agenda 21, endorsed at the United Nations Conference on Environment and Development in 1992. Sustainable development became the central axis of contemporary environmental discourses,[7] but it was criticised for conserving economic development rather than conserving environments.[8] Ecological modernisation then emerged as a step towards sustainable development, but it was also seen as an excuse for sustaining the structures and systems causing environmental decline.[9] Depending on your politics, ecological modernisation supported democratic experimentation[10] or it enabled big industry and big government to control more resources.[11] After ecological modernisation, carbon control emerged in the late 1990s as a solution to the much-talked-about global ecological threat of climate change. However, carbon control could be seen as potentially more regressive because of its reliance on moral and security imperatives sustained by apocalyptic imagery.[12] Either way you look at it, over the last forty years this talk of human-induced ecological threats has become normal. Perhaps the best-known speaker of these threats is the USA's former vice president Al Gore. His popular documentary, *An Inconvenient Truth*,[13] demanded that society be re-regulated to avoid its own doom through the apocalyptic scenario of human-induced climate change. During his Nobel Prize acceptance speech, it became apparent that Gore's campaign for global re-regulation of society favoured entrepreneurs and inventors.[14] Could this have been a sophisticated campaign to accelerate business as usual? Dutch scholar Maarten Hajer alluded to this type of political action when he detected a shift in environmental politics in the second half of the twentieth century, from a focus on the existence of an environmental problem to complex struggles over the meaning of an environmental problem.[15] As society became saturated with environmental discourse and nostalgia for remembered environments, it became more rational to demand reforms in the face of ecological threats. The most talked about, in recent times, being human-induced climate-change apocalypse.

Despite the pervasive talk of global ecological crisis, we do not sense ecological threats at a global scale. Instead, ecological threats are sensed in relation to our experiences of the world.[16] They may be sensed in relation to the regrettable loss of a familiar tree, the acrid smell of a factory at dawn or perhaps the multi-coloured plastic junk accumulating along a riverbank. Ecological crisis feels real in our own environmental worlds, but not so real at Earth scale. In understanding how people are moved or not moved by the prospect of ecological crisis, we should consider that the global ecological threats described by science are about as abstract as the planet named Earth. This is perhaps why international attempts to steer environmental discourse[17] have been frustrated by the multitude of local views on global ecological crisis. Environmental concerns can be exploited for international political strategies, and they also remain a powerful local stimulant. Concerns about near environments can unify a localised population against the threat of radical environmental change – even when this change is presented as a local solution to global ecological crisis.

North Port Quay was situated, initially, by news media as a potentially divisive issue for the 2008 Western Australian election. The state's premier, Alan Carpenter, and attorney general, Jim McGinty, were against the project while opposition Liberal leader Troy Buswell and shadow planning minister Simon O'Brien favoured exploring its merits.[18] Buswell said Carpenter's negativity to this 'visionary project' suggested the government lacked vision. North Port Quay enjoyed the support of *The West Australian*'s editorial page.[19] The newspaper reported that 'Perth's leading property developers and wealthiest businessmen' behind the $10 billion North Port Quay plan had launched a 'scathing attack on the state government' for shooting down the project.[20] Lobbyist John Halden said he had 'never seen a more put-your-head-in-the-sand approach from politicians', who feared debate and the election cycle in 'rejecting a project that would lead the world in environmentally friendly development'. The consortium released a poll, suggesting that 58 per cent of residents in Fremantle and Cottesloe wanted a new marina. Despite Halden's lobbying efforts for North Port Quay, his media appearances tended to taint the project, particularly his reported[21] association with cabinet leaks and practices that could be read as corrupting the state government. Halden, a former Labor Party State secretary and Upper House MP, was named by journalist Robert Taylor as the 'go-to man for businesses seeking access to all levels of government'.[22] An investigation was underway into the lobbying practices of Halden and other former Labor ministers such as Brian Burke, who was already tainted by corruption around the Smiths Beach property development. Locally, McGinty and Liberal MP Colin Barnett were united across party lines in rejecting North Port Quay.

The West Australian's letter page[23] suggested that most people supported North Port Quay, despite some dissent and a general wariness of spectacular coastal property developments. North Port Quay would be a Western Australian asset despite opposition by 'doomsdayers from the Premier down' who 'say it will be the end of civilization as we know it, the sky will fall in, the waves will wash away everything and it will be an environmental disaster'. This 'showcase for environmental sustainability using wind, wave and solar energy' would make Perth 'a world-class landmark'. Public support for the project was framed around the importance of developing the tourism sector to enable 'our beautiful country' to survive international economic competition once it had exhausted its stocks of natural resources. Dissent against the project was represented as the frustration of seeing funds 'poured into such an extravagant proposal when it was clearly not in the best interest of West Australians'. It would encroach on 'the wonderful, vibrant city of Fremantle'. Fremantle was represented as an ideal place and community – a utopia within Perth's dull metropolis – threatened by 'tragedy if this abhorrent development were to degrade' them in any way. The semiotic distinction between defending natural environments and defending urban environments clouded as Fremantle was talked about as something natural to be saved from the threat of an alien city.

An advertisement[24] for North Port Quay appeared in state and local newspapers within a week of the media launch. The background image in this half-page advertisement suggested motorboat amusement in a city by the water. Over this image was 'An Open Letter from the Boating Fraternity of Western Australia' supporting the project. There was a long list of project features, starting with the 'World's First Carbon-Free Development' and ending with 'Restaurants and Cafes'.

Articles on the project covered the front pages of the local weekly newspapers.[25] The *Fremantle Herald* reported a political storm raging over the scale and style of North Port Quay that would 'see publicly owned seabed reclaimed' for a project that would 'more than double the size of Fremantle'.[26] The newspaper alleged that Planning Minister Alannah MacTiernan's fingerprints were 'all over controversial plans for a Dubai-style island development worth billions at Rous Head in North Fremantle':

> Sustainability gun-for-hire Peter Newman told the *Herald* Ms MacTiernan told the developers to scale back their original proposal by more than half. This in turn led to 20-storey buildings and much higher density to house an expected 20,000 new residents.
>
> "Alannah's advice was to bring it back, she told them not to take it to her unless it was a third of the size," the Fremantle local and professor – a former WA government advisor and Labor insider – said of the proposal that has been in the pipeline for a number of years.[27]

A supporting image showed a lone male surfer – the icon of Fremantle Football Club – supposedly pondering the consortium's offer of a new surf break to replace the one he would lose in the photograph. Below this image, a headline boasted: 'Green city an Oz first'. Apparently, North Port Quay would be a 'green city' – 'the first carbon-neutral development in Australia'. Professor Newman was the only source and his expert position was beyond question within this article, but not without it. In another article, the *Herald* reported[28] '*howls* of protest' greeting developers who had 'their sights on a huge slice of seabed off Rous Head'. Among them, Greens MLC Paul Llewellyn apparently quipped: 'While Venice is sinking into the sea we're planning the next Venice in Perth'. Most ordinary members of Fremantle community seemed to be against the project. The *Fremantle Gazette*[29] suggested that the most credible local supporter of the project was 'Curtin University professor of sustainability, concept consultant and Fremantle resident Peter Newman'. Meanwhile, the Fremantle Society would rally against the project because there was no need to sacrifice people's beaches for urban development. The Save Freo Beaches Alliance was positioned in opposition to this privatisation of the seabed. So was the Greens party, which 'supported genuinely sustainable development' but not a 'fanciful' Venetian project facing rising sea levels.

Support for the project appeared to be more sustained at the state level. *The West Australian* presented various sources in favour of North Port Quay:[30] Tourism Council WA CEO, Graham Moss, supported this 'environmentally friendly opportunity to develop a world-class facility'; marine broker Brendon Grieve repeated what the boating fraternity had written in North Port Quay's advertisements; and boat-owner Richard Zandvliet lashed out at Alan Carpenter for rejecting this progressive project that would provide 2,200 'desperately needed' boat pens: 'here's the land and the ocean, it's completely degraded, let's do something with it'. Zandvliet was presented as a victim of Carpenter's dismissal of North Port Quay. Zandvliet couldn't secure a boat pen for 'his 36-foot yacht currently languishing on the hard stand' nor 'a special floating pen to accommodate his disabled daughter'. 'Give project a chance' was the headline over a North Port Quay image on the letters page of *The West Australian* on 4 June.[31] The project should be given a chance because it was visionary. North

Port Quay was written about as a progressive historical event, like the opening of the Swan River's mouth to clear the way for ships to dock at Fremantle's inner harbour. Experts of the 1890s against harbour construction turned out to be wrong, just as those against North Port Quay would be proven wrong in future, argued one letter writer. Another argued that the project would be swept off its sand foundation by the harsh sea environment, and that it would interfere with the port and cause 'untold environmental damage'.[32] Only an engineer without knowledge of the local coastal environment would have suggested building an 'ocean-based suburb off Fremantle'.[33] Another letter, 'Let them have it', parodied against 'the rich people' who could afford to build higher and higher sea walls and rebuild their houses if they were destroyed by rising sea levels.[34] Global ecological threats were merged with local threats in a limits-to-growth argument stacked against North Port Quay. The planet's depleted ecological capacity could just not sustain such 'extravagant developments'.[35] The project was described as an 'obscene and grubby' grab for limited resources that should be shared with 'ordinary working families of WA' who must 'contend with the hostile environment of the rising cost of living on every front'.[36] Resource limits and sustainable-development demands were associated with rising food, fuel and housing prices as well as demands for fair distribution of resources. The solution to local 'street violence, vandalism and criminal behaviour' caused by people being disenfranchised 'from sharing in the prosperity of a society' was 'better schools and hospitals'; which would do more to 'dispel the "Dullsville" tag' of Perth than 'some Dubai-style resort'.[37] North Port Quay's association with a Dubai resort could be read as a foreign attempt to impose more social injustice on the Western Australian community. Instead of spending billions of dollars 'creating land that only a few will be able to afford to live on', why not invest in agricultural technologies to 'sustain us beyond oil and climate change'?[38] North Port Quay's funding was becoming a discursive resource in arguing for investment in alternatives that would yield greater public goods within the context of depleting natural resources; the limits argument upon which sustainable development was constructed. On 5 June, a cartoon inside the cover of *The West Australian* reproduced concerns that North Port Quay was an obscene playground for the rich being designed behind closed doors by a handful of dodgy developers.

Lobbying for North Port Quay was *Fremantle Herald*'s top story on 7 June.[39] It described former Western Australian Premier Peter Dowding helping the consortium as an unpaid lobbyist 'to contact Fremantle movers and shakers the week before the electrifying project was unveiled'. The article discussed whether Dowding's lobbying business was improving due to 'the fall from grace of lobbyists Burke, Julian Grill and John Halden (all former parliamentary colleagues)'. Below this article was a large photograph of the abandoned Fremantle power station, captioned to remind readers of past efforts to keep developers' hands off Fremantle: 'The battle to save the Fremantle power station was thought to have been fought and won years ago, but now it's off the interim heritage register and could once again be at the mercy of developers.' To the left of this image an article described 'a swift and thunderous response to last week's lead story on the massive housing marina'. On page 2,[40] Peter Newman explained in an opinion piece that he had not gained personally from his role as North Port Quay's sustainability advisor. Professor Newman tackled criticism of his role head on:

> That this innovation requires debate is obvious but it
> should not descend into suggestions that the sustainability

components are just some greenwash and that expertise is being sought for purely private gain.[41]

Newman argued that it was more important that innovative experiments in sustainability such as this 'carbon-free development' proceed in approaching 'a carbon-constrained future'. Besides presenting competition for carbon resources, Newman framed the project within a competition for cultural capital: 'Perth has an opportunity to become a global leader due to this visionary concept'.[42] This sentence turned up again in a 'Myth Versus Fact' advertisement for North Port Quay in the same day's edition of *The West Australian* and, later, in the *Fremantle Gazette*.[43] The exact reproduction of this sentence suggested that Newman's representation of independence was somehow produced in consultation with North Port Quay's public-relations people. Directly below Newman's 'no personal gain' piece, the *Herald* published a press release from Strzelecki Holdings' media contact, David Christison, on behalf of the consortium.[44] The press release attempted to defend Newman's reputation as a 'sustainability expert' and head of Curtin University Sustainability Policy (CUSP) Institute. The press release quoted project concept director Chris Carman describing Peter Newman's relationship in terms of the provision of advice without direct payment because any research funded by the project would be channelled through CUSP as scholarships. Letters in this edition suggested great scepticism among readers about technical experts and property-development projects. The first letter argued that the construction of buildings, seawall and infill would make the project's positive energy light years away: Newman should make his carbon neutrality calculations public.[45] The letter asked whether buildings exposed to the Indian Ocean's harsh environment could be sustainable and then argued that it was a crime against nature to build over the sea when so much land was available. Another reader asked how much money 'rich people' wanted and at what expense 'to the environment, public beach and community wishes'.[46] North Port Quay was associated with environmental damage caused by developers of other large coastal projects, such as the nearby Port Coogee development. An emergent, possibly racist, reaction called Newman to order by promoting population limits and by 'protecting the natural environment from cashed-up private developers and their friends'.[47] Another letter – 'No fake islands for Fremantle' – shouted: 'We have one planet, one Australian coastline. Go away!!!'[48] Above this letter, the *Herald* included a cartoon parodying 'Rooshead Project' in the perceived language of the consortium ('www. bigseabucks.com'): 'A wonderful concept in money-making with eco aspects tacked on to get the locals on side'.[49] Another letter appeared to ask Newman, 'why are boat slips for power boats such a prominent feature' if the concern was global warming and petroleum scarcity? The consortium responded to these and other objections through half-page newspaper advertisements,[50] headed 'North Port Quay' and 'Myth Versus Fact'. The advertisements set out to put the record straight for things said 'in the past few days' that the consortium considered widely inaccurate. The 'myth' list provided insight into what the project had meant for many readers:

- It will be overwhelmed if there is a tsunami or a rise in sea levels due to global warming.
- Venice is sinking. This will also sink over time.
- The scale of it is "over the top."
- It will become a gated community and an enclave for the rich.
- It is not compatible with the operations of the port of Fremantle.
- It will encroach on Fremantle and ruin what we already have.
- It's all about profit for the developers.

- It'll never happen (Premier Alan Carpenter).[51]

The West Australian moved on from the North Port Quay issue to other news stories in the second week of June 2008 but the project's discussion was sustained by Fremantle's press. 'It's a "world beater"' appeared on the front page of the *Gazette* on 10 June, reporting that Newman maintained that North Port Quay would be a world first.[52] The article emphasised Newman's credentials as 'professor of sustainability at Curtin University' and his position that the development would attract 20,000 people to Fremantle without 'affecting the city's heritage'.[53] Page 4 of the same edition reported Colin Barnett opposing the project because it would deny locals access to 'their beaches', compound local traffic problems and because the consortium did not own the site or have a government mandate to develop it.[54] WA Planning Minister Alannah MacTiernan was reportedly opposed to the project unless there was 'significant' community support for it. The *Herald*'s subsequent edition was headlined, 'Wide support for islands plan':

> The massive $10 billion North Port Quay proposal – a six-island development off Rous Head – has strong community support, according to a WA-wide survey.
>
> John Halden, high-profile lobbyist and spruiker for the proponents North Port Quay, said a survey of 407 people across the state by Patterson Market Research (the folk who do Westpoll) found 60 per cent would be happy for the development to go ahead if it got a tick on environmental and planning grounds.[55]

Despite this positive page-1 headline, scepticism of the project abounded inside the *Herald*. 'Adam McHugh, a Murdoch

University sustainability expert,' challenged NPQ's 'carbon-free assertion' by arguing that 'carbon-neutral claims needed to be tested against energy used to create the massive...development, not just the energy to run the completed project'.[56] The article constructed a dialectic in which Newman defended his position on the grounds of particular technologies to be employed while reiterating that he would not be working with the consortium unless it was intending to build a world-first, self-sustainable city. In opposition, McHugh argued that the consortium's fees 'posed a conflict of interest with Prof Newman's role at the university' and that the partnership should be reviewed by the university's ethics committee. Newman reportedly responded that 'to put such enterprises through an ethics committee would bog down – and potentially erode – much-needed university funding'.[57] The North Port Quay issue was turning into a public battle of sustainable-development expertise in which the weapons were not just scientific methodology and reasoning but also the credentials and interests of the scientific experts. The *Herald*'s letters[58] section became a key site in the struggle around North Port Quay for credible positioning of sustainable development expertise. Amid public complaints about the consortium's lobbying operation and developers' broken promises, Newman's credibility was under pressure. The construction of high-rise, high-density residences on beach fronts was an irreconcilable problem for many letter writers, and others were concerned that North Port Quay would bring social harm. The consortium fought back in mid June with a new series of half-page advertisements in the *Herald*, the *Gazette* and *The West Australian*. The advertisement attempted to shift the division forming between Fremantle folk and project proponents to a division between patriotic Western Australians and unnamed others. In bold letters, the advertisement asked, 'Why can't

Western Australia lead the world in sustainable development?'[59] The advertisement's images suggested coastal amenity, green technologies, a healthy environment for future generations and a fun urban coastal lifestyle. The bottom section of the advertisement contained an aerial rendering of North Port Quay and a sentence associating it with the term 'carbon free' – a relatively little-known assembly of words.[60] The advertisements were apparently directed at getting people used to a new type of green built environment: 'North Port Quay would create an entirely new, environmentally sustainable coastal development and could become the world's first carbon-free development.' This advertisement, or a modified version, was published in *The West Australian* on 14 and 21 June, the *Gazette* on 17 June and the *Herald* again on 28 June. The differences in the modified version included alternative photographs and an additional sentence: 'Imagine clean beaches, energy from the sun, the waves and the wind and an electric cart in every home'.[61] These advertisements asked their audiences to imagine ideal futures for themselves in an ecological modernist paradise: the world's best sustainable urban environment – a kind of Utopia or new Atlantis – with abundant clean energy, clean beaches and abundant leisure time for clean family living. Nobody would work or be stuck in traffic in this urban, post-industrial, coastal paradise. Everybody would be healthy, wealthy and white.

Notes

1   *Fremantle Gazette*, 17 June 2008, p. 11.
2   J. D. Hughes, 'Early Greek and Roman environmentalists', in L. J. Bilsky (ed), *Historical Ecology: Essays on Environment and Social Change*, Kennikat Press, Port Washington, 1980, pp. 45–59.
3   R. T. Malthus, 'An Essay on the Principle of Population: The Sixth Edition (1826) with Variant Readings from the Second Edition (1803)', in E. A. Wrigley & D. Souden (eds), *The Works of Thomas Robert Malthus*, William Pickering, London, 1986.

4   P. P. Rogers, K. F. Jalal & J. A. Boyd, *An Introduction to Sustainable Development*, Earthscan, London, 2008.

5   D. H. Meadows, D. L. Meadows, J. Randers & W. W. Behrens III, *The Limits to Growth: a Report for the Club of Rome's Project on the Predicament of Mankind*, Universe Books, New York, 1972.

6   World Commission on Environment and Development, *Our Common Future*, Oxford University Press, Oxford, 1987.

7   J. S. Dryzek, *The Politics of the Earth: Environmental Discourses*, Oxford University Press, Oxford, 2005.

8   W. Sachs, 'In the wake of Rio', in W. Sachs (ed.), *Global Ecology: A New Arena of Political Conflict*, Fernwood Publishing, Halifax, 1993, pp. 3–21.

9   S. Young, 'The origins and evolving nature of ecological modernization', in S. Young (ed.), *The Emergence of Ecological Modernization: Integrating the Environment and the Economy?*, Routledge, London, 2000, pp. 1–40.

10 Dryzek, *The Politics of the Earth*, pp. 232–4.

11 D. Harvey, *Justice, Nature, and the Geography of Difference*, Blackwell Publishers, Cambridge, Massachusetts, 1996.

12 A. While, A. E. G. Jonas, & D. Gibbs, 'From sustainable development to carbon control: eco-state restructuring and the politics of urban and regional development', *Transactions of the Institute of British Geographers*, vol. 35, no. 1, 2010, pp. 76–93.

13 A. Gore, *An Inconvenient Truth*, Paramount Home Entertainment, Australia, 2006.

14 A. Gore, *Nobel Lecture*, Nobel Media, Stockholm, 2007, viewed 1 August 2008, <http://nobelprize.org/nobel_prizes/peace/laureates/2007/gore-lecture_en.html>.

15 M. A. Hajer, *The Politics of Environmental Discourse: Ecological Modernization and the Policy Process*, Oxford University Press, Oxford, 1995.

16 T. Kerr, 'Representing ecological threats and negotiating green built environments', PhD thesis, Curtin University, 2012, pp. 219–50.

17 Representations of ecological crisis are often encountered through the mediated reproduction of governmental and global institutional discourses. The Intergovernmental Panel on Climate Change (IPCC) was created in 1988 to reproduce ecological threat representations for a global media audience. S. H. Schneider, S. Semenov, A. Patwardhan, I. Burton, C. H. D. Magadza, M. Oppenheimer, et al. 'Assessing key vulnerabilities and the risk from climate change', in M. L. Parry, O. F. Canziani, J. P. Palutikof, P. J. van der Linden & C. E. Hanson (eds), *Climate Change 2007: Impacts, Adaptation and Vulnerability*, Cambridge University Press, Cambridge, 2007, pp. 779–810.

18   *The West Australian*, 30 May 2008, p. 9.
19   Ibid., p. 20.
20   *The West Australian,* 31 May 2008, p 2.
21   Ibid., pp. 6–7.
22   Ibid.
23   Ibid., p. 22.
24   Ibid., p. 61. This advertisement would appear again in subsequent days in the *Fremantle Gazette* and *Fremantle Herald*.
25   *Fremantle Herald,* 31 May 2008, p. 1; *Fremantle Gazette*, 3 June 2008, p. 1.
26   *Fremantle Herald,* 31 May 2008, p. 1.
27   Ibid.
28   Ibid., p. 3.
29   *Fremantle Gazette*, 3 June 2008, p. 1.
30   *The West Australian*, 2 June 2008, p. 3.
31   *The West Australian*, 4 June 2008, p. 22.
32   Ibid.
33   Ibid.
34   Ibid.
35   Ibid.
36   Ibid.
37   Ibid.
38   Ibid.
39   *Fremantle Herald*, 7 June 2008, p. 1.
40   Ibid., p. 2.
41   Ibid.
42   Ibid.
43   *The West Australian*, 7 June 2008, p. 62; Fremantle Gazette, 10 June 2008, p. 15.
44   *Fremantle Herald*, 7 June 2008, p. 2.
45   Ibid., p. 4.
46   Ibid.
47   Ibid.
48   Ibid.
49   Ibid.
50   *The West Australian*, 7 June 2008, p. 62; *Fremantle Gazette*, 10 June 2008, p. 15.
51   Ibid.
52   *Fremantle Gazette*, 10 June 2008, p. 1.
53   Ibid.
54   Ibid.
55   *Fremantle Herald*, 14 June 2008, p. 1.

56 Ibid.
57 Ibid.
58 *Fremantle Herald*, 14 June 2008, pp. 4–6.
59 Ibid., p. 7.
60 A Google search on 2 November 2009 produced 8,600,000 listings for 'carbon neutral' and only 402,000 for 'carbon free'.
61 *Fremantle Gazette*, 17 June 2008, p. 11.

POWER

Photograph by author

'I turned back to focus on the beautiful creatures, just in time to see her squirt water into the air, as if to say hello.'[1]

Tani Garden

People are moved by sensory experience. This is overlooked in everyday, apparently rational discussions of contemporary society. If we enjoy the shade of a particular tree, we may be moved to anger by the arrival of a bulldozer to destroy it. However, 'it' is not the tree that we are moved to protect; 'it' is experience of the tree: escaping heat in its shade, savouring its smell, hearing birds in its branches, a friend's laughter nearby, rough bark on skin.

Whereas we may not pay much attention to news of a company gaining a timber concession to a distant forest, we are likely to be antagonised by the arrival of a bulldozer threatening our sensual experience of a familiar tree. This is the key to understanding environmental politics in a case such as North Port Quay.

This potential power of sensory experience was overlooked by Fremantle's Mayor Peter Tagliaferri in the environmental politics around North Port Quay. Soon after its launch, Tagliaferri commended the project for its planned extension of Fremantle harbour, for its potential to increase municipal rates by $10 million and for making 15 per cent of its residences available for public housing.[2] Initially, Fremantle Council was divided over North Port Quay. The mayor and Councillors Robert Fittock, Bill Massie and Doug Thompson were reportedly in favour of the project, whereas Councillors Jon Strachan, Brad Pettitt, Les Lauder, Donna Haney and John Dowson were against it.[3] A year later, this council would act in response to a localised popular movement against North Port Quay. Fremantle Council's motion against the project came about because citizens' subjectivity to the sensory experience of local places affected the politics around North Port Quay. This was about the power of proximity − when environmental risks threaten local, beloved places − played out through Fremantle's media, public meetings and elections.

For the radical North Port Quay development to appear environmentally friendly, it was presented to the Western Australian public as a solution to a future global ecological crisis. But this positioning failed, as many people in Fremantle saw their local environment being threatened by the construction of North Port Quay. Proponents positioned North Port Quay as a world-class sustainable development for controlling future carbon emissions. When they spoke of carbon control they referenced global community. When they spoke of sustainable development it was in relation to global, national, state and the broad metropolitan community of Perth. Their opponents saw the project as a looming environmental threat to Port, Leighton and Cottesloe beaches, Rous Head, Fremantle Port and other local places. North Port Quay's initial PR materials avoided referencing these local places by associating the project with broader geographies. North Port Quay dominated the foreground of its PR video simulation, while Fremantle, Leighton and Cottesloe were blurred until almost unrecognisable in the background. In constructing a sense of controversy around the project's launch, television news producers introduced opposition by cutting to scenes of beaches and other local places around Fremantle. Positioning the project in its immediate spatial context was essential to the media construction of controversy around the project. This shifted the project's spatial context from global to local settings, and its temporal context back from the future, which is where proponents attempted to locate it. Heroically, Professor Peter Newman stood by the project by trying to explain to increasingly sceptical audiences that the project would be a world-leading carbon-free development when measured by its future operational performance. 'North Port Quay is an innovative concept in urban development,' he said, 'which requires some significantly different thinking as we approach a carbon-constrained future.'[4] Yet, even if the project could become a solution for a carbon-constrained future as argued repeatedly by Newman, Fremantle audiences saw no solution in it for themselves. Instead they saw the project immediately aggravating climate change and threatening their local coastal environment. A desire to protect their aesthetic relations with this environment would unify public voices in Fremantle against the threat of this imposing mega development.

The promotional videos and renderings made available to the media portrayed North Port Quay through simulated video footage as though it were shot from a passing helicopter.[5] The North Port Quay future was represented as immaculate urbanism: there was no construction or industrial production in sight. No one walked or loitered on the empty streets of North Port Quay. Stout lines on beaches in the distance may have depicted people, but they were not in any way discernible, unlike the seagulls flying in the foreground of North Port Quay's video simulation. While this world-class sustainable development didn't seem to include people, the global ecological threats of climate change and carbon emissions were being addressed by hidden ecological modernisation technologies. Such images of North Port Quay did not contradict understandings of sustainable development at conferences and meetings in other parts of Australia and North America, according to Newman.[6] Locally, however, the intended meaning for North Port Quay was disrupted by locals' sensory experience of places around the proposed project site. The political battle over North Port Quay's meaning was won on the field of proximity by mobilising references of sensory experience.

The initial burst of advertising for North Port Quay referred to environmental issues at the scale of planet and state: 'Why can't Western Australia lead the world in sustainable development?' These large geographic scales for legitimising North Port Quay were initially taken up by some media; the *Fremantle Herald* celebrated the project on page 1 as 'the first carbon-neutral development in Australia'.[7] However, the tenability of positioning North Port Quay as a future solution to ecological threats at state, national or global level quickly deteriorated as other authorised voices in the media repositioned the project as an immediate threat to local places. The project was repositioned as an environmental threat by its representation in current time and space, near neighbourhood beaches and other local places. This shift in the representation of North Port Quay from an acceptable project to a rejectable project relied on the temporal and spatial context of the project being shifted from the distant future back to local immediacy.

Opposition voices tended to discuss the project in different spatial or temporal contexts. For example, the project was problematised in the local distant future by Fremantle Ports CEO Kerry Sanderson: 'the traffic chaos that would ensue from the additional 40,000 vehicle movements each day on the north Fremantle peninsula'.[8] It was problematised in the global immediate future because of carbon emissions from its site reclamation and construction, for example, by Murdoch University sustainability expert Adam McHugh.[9] North Port Quay also appeared as an imminent, local threat to Fremantle's culture within public talk that saw the project provoking the sea's destructive power: 'If this development is allowed to go ahead, you will lose your beaches, surf clubs and restaurants due to coastal erosion'.[10] In an early colonial building down the road from where transgressors used to be hung on Cliff Street, Andrew Smith and his staff at the *Fremantle Herald* sensed the local public's tide of conviction turning against North Port Quay and its proponents. The *Fremantle Herald* published more news on North Port Quay than any other newspaper. In a year and a half, the weekly newspaper published 438 articles, editorials, advertisements or letters referring to North Port Quay.[11] The *Herald*, a free weekly newspaper with a masthead describing itself as 'Fremantle's own INDEPENDENT newspaper', had a significant presence in Fremantle municipality and the state's Fremantle electorate. Its principal income source was advertising, mainly from real estate companies and property developers but also, significantly during this period, from candidates contesting political positions. The Circulations Audit Board recorded 81,960 copies of the *Herald* (including its Melville and Cockburn editions) being delivered to letterboxes each week around the time of North Port Quay's launch compared to 64,179 copies of News Corporation's *Fremantle Gazette, Cockburn Gazette* and *Melville Times*.[12] Both the *Fremantle Herald* and *Fremantle Gazette* were distributed for free through letterboxes, newsagents and cafes around Fremantle. *Fremantle Herald*'s director and chief editor – the baseball-capped Andrew Smith – knew his newspaper's survival depended on local controversy, elections and real estate. He would not miss the opportunity of this triad coinciding around North Port Quay for the newspaper's benefit. Within a few weeks of the project's launch, the *Fremantle Herald* started to drive home the emerging meaning of North Port Quay as a threat to his readers' sense of beach culture. Over an inside-front-page spread in its 28 June 2008 edition, a headline exclaimed: 'NPQ to block views of Rotto'.[13] This headline ran over a two-page altered photograph of the view from Port Beach to Rottnest Island. The altered image showed North Port Quay's seawall and buildings blocking a view from the beach to the island. The NPQ consortium was reportedly preparing to spend $100 million to lease the 345-hectare seabed site. Once reclaimed as land, this site reportedly would be worth over a billion dollars. The project's PR person, Ann Burns, seemed confident, pointing to the state government's demonstrated willingness to flog off nearby ocean bed. On the same page, the mayor of Cottesloe, Kevin Morgan, warned that sand erosion from North Port Quay could mean the end of iconic Cottesloe Beach.[14] 'People who value those beaches,' he said, 'ought to be concerned'.[15] Threats to local beach environments from North Port Quay were not merely threats to nature; they were threats to the idea of beach culture shaped by people's sensory experience of days, and perhaps fun nights, at the beach. This integration of feeling into thinking supported popular calls for the project to be prevented.

'We, the working Western Australians, cannot live by the beach in expensive suburbs but have always had the free beaches and the free horizon to go to escape suburbia,' wrote A. M. Collins in the *Fremantle Herald*.[16] 'If this blot is built, instead of getting away from our ordinary suburbs we will be able to go to the beach and see a suburb in the sea where other people live in housing we can't afford.'[17] The threats to the people's environment from North Port Quay were associated with other problems caused by coastal property development projects, such as sand-dune erosion at the Port Coogee development to the south of Fremantle, and to general experiences of pollution and disruption around construction projects. 'Who wants to spend time on a beach watching and listening to barges trundling along?' asked Marion Blair. 'How many are needed? How many a day for how long? And where is the material coming from?'[18] The environmental problems associated with North Port Quay were related to local coastal experiences. The threat of this development disrupting the vista from Port Beach, for instance, was viewed as a threat to what people could see and otherwise sense in the immediate environment. 'I saw a whale the other day at Port Beach, North Fremantle,' wrote Tani Garden, 'close enough to point out to my 3-year-old twin boys. They saw its fin and tail splash out of the water and I thought how lucky we were'.[19] When Tani Garden looked towards Rous Head and tried to imagine the high-rise buildings of North Port Quay, she couldn't picture it: 'it was all too ugly and destroying the moment I was having with the whale... I turned back to focus on the beautiful creatures, just in time to see her squirt water into the air, as if to say hello.' Tani said, 'experiences like this are sacred'.[20] Such threats to the sensory experiences of citizens unified a discursive frontier[21] against North Port Quay, behind which a variety of citizens' demands aggregated in popular defence of local beaches. The Greens candidate, Adele Carles, would contribute to this emerging popular front against coastal property development in the 2008 state-election campaign, which she started work on within weeks of the launch of North Port Quay. Carles would take to the beach in long black boots and suit skirt to declare, 'Fremantle is under siege'. [22] She told the local public that they could lose what was special about Fremantle: 'Social, heritage and community are all up for grabs,' she said from the beach. 'We are against seabed being privatised – it's an insult to the Australian way of life.' Carles cleverly drew on the potential political power of beach aesthetics. 'We love our views of Rottnest,' she campaigned on the cover of *Fremantle Herald*[23] a month before the state election was called.

Notes

1   *Fremantle Herald,* 7 June 2008, p. 6.
2   *Fremantle Herald*, 21 June 2008, p. 7.
3   Ibid.
4   *Fremantle Herald*, 7 June 2008, p. 2.
5   'WA Premier criticises Fremantle island plan', ABC News WA, Perth, 29 May 2008.
6   *Fremantle Herald*, 27 June 2009, p. 6.
7   *Fremantle Herald*, 31 May 2008, p. 1.
8   *Fremantle Herald*, 12 July 2008, p. 1.
9   *Fremantle Herald*, 14 June 2008, p. 2.
10   *Fremantle Herald*, 21 June 2008, p. 4.
11   T. Kerr, 'Representing ecological threats and negotiating green built environments', PhD thesis, Curtin University, 2012, p. 91.
12   *Fremantle Herald*, 18 October 2008, p. 1.
13   *Fremantle Herald*, 28 June 2008, pp. 2–3.
14   Ibid., p. 3.
15   Ibid.

16 *Fremantle Herald*, 28 June 2008, p. 15.
17 Ibid.
18 *Fremantle Herald*, 5 July 2008, p. 4.
19 *Fremantle Herald*, 7 June 2008, p. 6.
20 Ibid.
21 A theoretical approach to the formation of such frontiers has been developed by E. Laclau, *On Populist Reason*, Verso, London, 2005, pp. 76–115.
22 *Fremantle Herald*, 5 July 2008, p. 1.
23 Ibid.

STATE ELECTION

Greens campaign advertisement, as it appeared in *Fremantle Herald*

'The boldness of the [North Port Quay] plan is impressive. It could only be made a reality though if the engineering, social and environmental issues were satisfactorily addressed...These kinds of projects deserve to at the very least be investigated and properly considered rather than arrogantly dismissed out of hand as the Premier has done'[1]

Opposition Liberal Leader Troy Buswell

'To create an offshore city of 20,000 people there could have unforseen ramifications for our coastline, while denying the people of the southern suburbs their beaches...Let's remember

that it is not as if they own the land or sea bed, have won a
government mandate to develop it, or the right to lease the land'[2]
Future Liberal Leader and Premier Colin Barnett

Standing against North Port Quay was a confident step in the leadership comeback of Colin Barnett, who had resigned as leader of the Liberal party in Western Australia in 2005 after losing the state election. By late 2007, it seemed as though Barnett would resign from politics altogether.[3] But, instead of quitting, Barnett seized the day on 6 August 2008 to be elected unopposed as party leader. Troy Buswell had resigned from the post two days earlier amid mounting media pressure for gesturing and groping at the private parts of people on both sides of politics.[4] Then a day after Barnett's return as Liberal leader, Labor Premier Alan Carpenter called a state election for 6 September, six months ahead of schedule. Against a shrewd Barnett, it seemed that the Labor Government's days were numbered.

North Port Quay was tied up in Western Australian politics because such a radical development could only proceed with a supportive state government and approvals from its statutory agencies. From the outset, Liberal Leader Troy Buswell and Shadow Planning Minister Simon O'Brien appeared cautiously in support of the project, while Labor Premier Alan Carpenter and Attorney General Jim McGinty were steadfastly against.[5] Colin Barnett did his own thing, immediately breaking ranks with Buswell's shadow cabinet on North Port Quay. He stood – in blue shirtsleeves on the beach in his electorate of Cottesloe – firmly against the threat of this seabed development. The Greens in the neighbouring electorate of Fremantle adopted a similar position, standing repeatedly on the beach as true defenders against coastal property development and reminding voters of Labor's history

of failing to defend public beaches and dunes from encroach-
ment by property developers. Labor's planning minister Alannah
MacTiernan had a reputation for supporting big coastal property
developments and she seemed ambivalent about North Port Quay.

Sensing opportunity, the Greens' campaign for local seats in
the 2008 state election opened early. The front page of *Fremantle
Herald*'s 5 July edition was headlined 'Greens see change: Battle for
the beaches "may turn tide"'. A photograph of the Greens' local
women, Adele Carles and Lynn MacLaren, suggested a future
victory on the beach, in defence of beaches. The electoral tide was
shifting their way from Labor, which had held Fremantle for the
better part of a century. Adele Carles, who had run an enterprising
campaign as a Coastal Independent against property development
at South Beach, was positioned as the person to knock Labor's
Fremantle incumbent, Jim McGinty, off his perch:

> With pollsters predicting a swing against the Liberal
> party and a swing to Greens in this election, Liberal
> preferences could nudge the Greens over the line in
> Fremantle – fuelled by anger over development plans
> such as three harbours, Victoria Quay and now North
> Port Quay.[6]

The developers of North Port Quay tried to disrupt the public
mood against the project by commissioning another survey by
Patterson Market Research which showed that most people still
supported some of the things offered in a project like North
Port Quay. However, several survey respondents contacted the
Fremantle Herald to complain about leading questions in the
Patterson telephone survey. The developers' attempt to represent
public opinion quickly turned into resentment of their attempted

manipulation of opinion, according to the *Herald* which published dozens of reader letters against North Port Quay. This apparent groundswell of public opinion against the project, however, faltered when only fifty or so people turned up at an anti-NPQ rally in Fremantle's Esplanade Park outside the historical Esplanade Hotel, where a community briefing was being held by the proponents of North Port Quay:

> While the small but vocal group shouted "POQ NPQ" outside the Esplanade Hotel, inside 132 attended a forum on the 345-hectare development.
>
> From the hotel entry NPQ's PR man David Christison and the group's sustainability expert Peter Newman watched on smiling before walking back inside.[7]

Liberal candidate for Alfred Cove Chris Back was at the briefing. Like his party leader Troy Buswell, Dr Back publicly supported 'further study of the project, including wide community consultation, environmental-impact assessment and an economic-feasibility study prior to any decision being taken on whether to move ahead.'[8] His position was distinguished against the 'out of hand' rejection of North Port Quay by Labor Premier Alan Carpenter and his Attorney General Jim McGinty.

Adele Carles said there were 100 protestors at the rally, sending 'a clear message that privatising the seabed was not an acceptable option'. 'We want to see these ridiculous plans shelved once and for all,' she said. 'I encourage NPQ to demonstrate its environmental credentials and commitment by creating a carbon-neutral suburb on land.'[9] Adele's husband, Francois Carles, told the press his family had watched North Port Quay's promotional DVD with disbelief. He said it looked like a fantasy movie featuring tropical fish in marine parks where fishing was banned, not the sort of fish that were endangered by fishing around Fremantle.[10] Lynn MacLaren asked why the seabed should be sold for less than floor tiles at $27.30 a square metre. She also asked why the public had 'to wait 10 years, privatise our seabed, and build 345ha of islands' just to tackle climate change and housing afford-ability? But public contests are as much about showing support as they are about demonstrating argument. North Port Quay's project manager, Chris Carman, maintained the anti-NPQ rally drew only 53 protesters against 'broad public support for this bold and visionary concept for a truly sustainable development'.[11] Real estate agent Nik Varga chimed in to support the project. Meanwhile, Carles argued the NPQ picket was not a flop: 'John Halden, NPQ's lobbyist, certainly wasn't smiling smugly with sustainability advisor Peter Newman – we saw him running for cover.'[12] Carles said, 'NPQ is attempting to win public opinion with the misleading advertising it is disseminating. This plan is a distraction from the real challenges we face. The twin problems of global warming and peak oil are here,' she told the press. 'We want genuine sustainable development now – our government has done a lot of talking about renewable energy, public transport, green buildings, walkable neighbourhoods, liveable cities,' she said. 'We must now act. I can't look my children in the eye and tell them that we, "the adults", are onto this because we're not.'[13] Carles closed the proximity of ecological threats around North Port Quay while appealing for public action in the name of motherhood: threats must be dealt with here and now by the people and their government for children's sakes. By framing the threat as local, and soliciting emotion by referencing motherhood, Carles undermined North Port Quay's suggested rationale that environmental problems were located in the future in the form of carbon-emission constraints. Motherhood and close proximity of environmental threats were deployed in the Greens' local campaign advertising for the state election. The Greens called on citizens to vote green to protect 'our remaining parks and open space', 'our beaches and coastal foreshores', and 'our children'.[14] Adele Carles and Lynn MacLaren were advertised standing on Port Beach near the proposed site of North Port Quay. They stood for local rail transport, affordable housing and support for public teachers, nurses and doctors. They stood against lead-carbonate exports through Fremantle port and against coastal property development projects, particularly housing over the sea.

Within this intense public debate about coastal property development before the state election, Professor Peter Newman maintained that North Port Quay would be an important step in changing government policy in the face of peak oil and climate change. 'If companies can demonstrate how to be carbon-free, especially oil-free, then markets will take over and drag governments with them,' he said.[15] North Port Quay 'is big and bold enough to influence far beyond the local. I don't for a moment believe its developers are working for purely idealistic beliefs, just as I know governments aren't'.

The stakes were high, and extending corporate power over democratic institutions was apparently integral to this bold sustainability project, Newman said. 'The project is not pure and perfect, but it is a great opportunity for significant demonstration of the carbon-constrained future.' Peter Newman also talked about North Port Quay being motivated by 'the needs of people similar to those who came' for the America's cup. These arriving colonists knew what they wanted, according to Newman: 'They want a small city for boat-oriented people. They also want a legacy,' he said. 'They chose a site that hasn't been pristine ocean for 100 years.'[16] While Newman drew attention to what 'they' wanted, Carles solicited 'our' desires. Fremantle locals parodied Newman's approach, one calling it the 'predicted story of the very beginning of the New Land (NPQ)' for 'my children (the Great Unwashed of present-day Fremantle)'.[17] Another pointed to a 'Terra Nullius' (a presumed empty land) approach to property development in Fremantle.[18] Indeed, North Port Quay's utopian promise – 'to build a sustainable new community'[19] – begged the question of what would happen to the good old community.

Two weeks ahead of the state election, the *Fremantle Herald* went to press with a special edition, entitled 'The development issue'.[20] It featured 59 major building projects planned for sites in and around Fremantle. Articles on page 2 and a map on page 3 showed readers what was 'in-store'. Mayor Tagliaferri predicted that Fremantle could become a 'real' city by 2020 with its population reaching 35,000, not including 20,000 people living in North Port Quay. To the south, Cockburn Mayor Stephen Lee was presiding over a bewildering array of developments to make that municipality a 'residential and industrial powerhouse'.[21] The *Herald*'s map suggested that about a third of Fremantle and Cockburn would be covered by these new developments, and that most of the coastline would be occupied by just a few of these property-development projects. Pollsters predicted that with 'thousands of people set to move into millionaire neighbourhoods along the coast from Fremantle to Cockburn, Labor's stranglehold is under threat'.[22] The demographic overwhelming of Labor voters was already underway, according to Murdoch University expert Ian Cook, but it would be exacerbated by North Port Quay. The project was seen as a much larger version of the recent Port Coogee development, where people had paid an average

$3.2 million per 500-square-metre block on 'seabed at the former industrial backwater'.[23] The Greens candidate for Cockburn Andrew Sullivan drove this point home in distinguishing his party from the major parties:

> The proponents want to fill in an area of ocean 10 times larger than Port Coogee, engulfing much of Port Beach in the process.
>
> They obviously think they can get around the some- what apologetic promise made by Alannah MacTiernan that the likes of Port Coogee will never happen again. Perhaps their ex-Labor lobbyists know all too well how to circumvent the stated opposition from both Carpenter and Barnett.[24]

Sullivan, an architect and known coastal campaigner, used North Port Quay as a benchmark for wastage and unfair resource distribution:

> …spending $2 billion filling in the ocean for housing is a hopelessly unsustainable extravagance. It is also environ- mentally irresponsible in the face of climate change and rising sea levels…If there's enough money in the system to spend billions of dollars on filling in the ocean for a few thousand well-heeled people, surely there's enough to build a train line through Cockburn that an entire community can prosper for generations to come.[25]

The sense of injustice in resource allocation articulated locally during the state election campaign was linked to diminishing local-community control over planning decisions since the 1990s, 'when it seemed that the battle to save our heritage buildings and streetscenes had been won'.[26] *Vox populi* responses to newspaper interviews suggested that property development was inevitable, but if it must happen it should not be 'too Americanised. We should aim for a more European way of life', said one respondent from Hamilton Hill.[27] Property development should be low-rise, visually appealing and done in a way that won't upset the 'Fremantle vibe', spoil beaches or cause parking problems, said other respondents.[28] Property development should be done in a way that looks after the environment and works for local businesses and community by responding to local voices of concern. Property development is fine, said Marianne Johnson on Fremantle's High Street, as 'long as we don't go and spoil the beaches, which should be for the people...I'm definitely against the North Port Quay development.'[29] The project was linked in meetings and the media to threats of overcrowding that would limit the spatial resources required for the 'Aussie way of life'[30] and damage 'our coast'.[31] The public mood was summed up by Fremantle letter-writer Charles Dortch: 'our beaches' were 'infinitely more important...than the narrowly focussed, though massive-scale investment interests'.[32] People were getting angry. Jim McGinty was accused of 'pre-election greenwash': feigning opposition to North Port Quay then dancing to the tune of a developer-driven state-planning depart-ment after the election.[33] 'NPQ spin doctors' were described as manufacturing public support in the lead up to a project submis-sion to the planning department.[34] Two weeks before the state election it was clear that North Port Quay was seen by credible locals as an environmental threat, not an environmental solution.

Peter Newman had the lonely task of defending the project a week out from the election. He argued that he did not use the word 'sustainability' lightly and that Fremantle's poorer past was not as rosy as some suggested. Being a backwater was not sustainable and offered nothing for young people, he argued. Newman responded to Jim McGinty's call to 'protect our beaches from NPQ' by arguing that the project would improve local beaches and create three additional beaches through proven engineering methods. He also responded to criticism of the need to build at sea by arguing that North Port Quay's '5-metre sea wall' would keep it safe from rising sea levels.[35] Meanwhile, the Save Freo Beaches Alliance asked newspaper readers to vote for candidates who opposed the development of coastal properties. The alliance's full-page advertisement suggested local constituents vote for candidates against North Port Quay to undermine the consortium's attempt to represent public support for the project: because the 'backers of the North Port Quay mega-development spruik its supposed environmental credentials and aim at "proving" public support before they take their proposal to the next State Government'.[36] Beaches were represented by the alliance as complex, fragile, natural systems relying on 'replenishment by wind, waves and currents that shift sand up the coast' which would be endangered by reclamation for housing projects. Rising sea levels were envisaged, threatening 30,000 buildings between Fremantle and Mandurah due to global warming, and the state Labor government's policies were represented as endangering rather than protecting buildings from these threats. The alliance said: 'Candidates for the state election on 6th Sept know the voting public want the coastline protected. Voters must ask whom they will trust to campaign on this issue beyond election day!'[37] According to the alliance, Greens and Labor candidates were preferred over local Liberal party candidates. Facing the alliance's full-page advertisement in *Fremantle Herald* on 30 August, another full-page advertisement linked the election to the defence of beaches. The Greens candidates Andrew Sullivan and

Adele Carles were advertised, apparently, at South Beach, the site of an enduring community struggle against property development. Reminiscent of Winston Churchill's rally to battle against Nazi Germany, the Greens declared: 'We Will Fight Them on the Beaches!' Carles and Sullivan were placed in an apparently similar heroic struggle against foreign aggression:

> Andrew & Adele have led brave and just public campaigns to defend our beaches from environmental and social vandalism.
>
> Each has faced slander, intimidation, threats of financial ruin and determined, aggressive campaigns of misinformation organized by some developers and their lackeys.
>
> The highly controversial Port Coogee and spectacularly uninspired South Beach developments ARE NOT PROGRESS. They are the irrevocable and disastrous results of a weak council and compliant WA government response to corporate pressure, against which a staunch but unequal battle is fought.
>
> WE MUST NEVER ALLOW THIS TO HAPPEN AGAIN!
>
> With Andrew and Adele as our local members, WE WILL FIGHT THEM ON THE BEACHES AND WIN![38]

The final incitement for local voters to think 'people power' against property development was delivered on the eve and morning of the state election with a headline on the front page of *Fremantle Herald* announcing: 'Prof: give Freo planning to state'. Reportedly, Peter Newman had told a North Port Quay forum that development planning for large projects should be handed to the state after the election because the local council wasn't up to this task. The article appeared directly above a photograph of a bulldozer demolishing a local heritage house that the state government had failed to protect. This image was on the mind of some voters as they headed into polling stations around Fremantle on that sunny Saturday in September.

The state election resulted in the Carpenter Labor Government being replaced by Colin Barnett's Liberal–National party coalition. It was seen as opening the way for new property-development projects around Fremantle. North Port Quay's project manager Chris Carman seemed optimistic as he prepared to approach the new government for development approval.[39] A higher-density future was envisaged for Fremantle and Perth, with the port facilities on Rous Head being overrun by skyscrapers.[40] The appointment of Simon O'Brien as transport minister was seen as increasing the chance of Fremantle's port facilities being relocated further south: 'Mr O'Brien first raised the idea last year when he announced his vision for North Quay to become a housing estate'.[41] Fremantle Mayor Peter Tagliaferri argued that Fremantle was defined by its port and its relocation could turn Fremantle into 'just another suburb': 'This is a once in a lifetime opportunity by the Liberals to destroy Fremantle,' declared the mayor.[42] Labor member Jim McGinty, who had just hung onto his seat, concurred that anything attacking the port also attacked Fremantle.

The election hadn't made life easier for the proponents of North Port Quay, who reportedly had amended the project plans to make them palatable for approval by 'the new Barnett Liberal government'.[43] However, the Fremantle Society's president, Ian Alexander, pledged to lobby the new premier, who was 'a long-standing member of the society'.[44] The Greens' anti-coastal-development campaign was seen as successful. It had helped Lynn MacLaren win a seat in the upper house of state parliament. In the lower house, Adele Carles came close to winning Fremantle, a traditionally safe Labor seat. Charismatic environmentalist Bob Brown announced national support from the Greens for Carles at the next election because she had won 'the highest-ever Green vote for a lower house seat in Australia'.[45] Adele Carles ran a long game, preparing immediately for the next election. 'Thank you for making Fremantle a very unsafe seat,' she told voters. 'We came close this time, stay with us. Next time we'll make history and break into the lower house of parliament for the first time.'[46]

Notes

1   *The West Australian*, 30 May 2008, p. 9.

2   *Fremantle Gazette*, 10 June 2008, p. 4.

3   'Barnett to quit politics', ABC, Sydney, 27 November 2007, viewed 7 April 2014, <http://www.abc.net.au/news/2007–11–27/barnett-to-quit-politics/970390>.

4   'Chair-sniffing Lib quits as leader', Sydney Morning Herald, Sydney, August 4, 2008, viewed 7 April 2014, <http://www.smh.com.au/news/national/chairsniffing-lib-quits-as-leader/2008/08/04/1217701922645.html>.

5   *The West Australian*, 30 May 2008, p. 9.

6   *Fremantle Herald*, 5 July 2008, p. 1.

7   *Fremantle Herald*, 19 July 2008, p. 2.

8   *Fremantle Gazette*, 29 July 2008, p. 1.

9   Ibid.

10 *Fremantle Herald*, 2 August 2008, p. 6.

11 *Fremantle Gazette*, 5 August 2008, p. 9.

12 *Fremantle Herald*, 9 August 2008, p. 4.

13 Ibid.

14 *Fremantle Herald*, 16 August 2008, p. 3.

15 Ibid., pp. 6–7.

16 Ibid.

17 *Fremantle Herald*, 4 October 2008, p. 16.

18 *Fremantle Herald*, 20 December 2008, p. 13.
19 *Fremantle Gazette*, 9 February 2009, pp. 24–25.
20 *Fremantle Herald*, 23 August 2008.
21 Ibid., p. 2.
22 Ibid., p. 5.
23 Ibid., p. 6.
24 Ibid., p. 9.
25 Ibid.
26 *Fremantle Herald*, 23 August 2008, p. 11.
27 Ibid., p. 12.
28 Ibid.
29 Ibid.
30 *Fremantle Herald*, 23 August 2008, p. 18.
31 *Fremantle Herald*, 30 August 2008, p. 17.
32 *Fremantle Herald*, 23 August 2008, p. 16.
33 Ibid.
34 Ibid.
35 *Fremantle Herald*, 30 August 2008, p. 6.
36 Ibid., p. 16.
37 Ibid.
38 *Fremantle Herald*, 30 August 2008, p. 17.
39 *Fremantle Herald*, 20 September 2008, p. 2.
40 Ibid., p. 1.
41 Ibid.
42 Ibid.
43 *Fremantle Herald*, 20 September 2008, p. 2.
44 Ibid.
45 *Fremantle Herald*, 3 January 2009, p. 8.
46 *Fremantle Herald*, 13 September 2008, p. 7.

GREEN BUILDING

Photograph by author

'North Port Quay aims to combine all these innovations to build a sustainable new community.'[1]

North Port Quay

'…not only planned, but it is planned with a view to the very latest of modern requirements…'[2]

Ebenezer Howard

Green buildings of the twenty-first century seem fragmented, transparent, and excessively spacious. They appear to have broken out of the compartmentalising black-box boundaries of postmodernist architecture best described in Los Angeles' Bonaventure Hotel. Pass through T3 at Singapore airport and you may not sense the enclosure of its distant ceiling and glass walls. The building openly simulates nature. Not through its interior gardens, but through its excess space, absence of discernible boundaries and the seemingly unknowable logic of its moving parts. It's an artificial butterfly garden in there, and you appreciate it all the more when encountering the solid white walls of Perth's international airport. Those interior walls suggest the hard reality of constructed national boundaries, which feels wholly unnatural after a Singapore T3 experience.

Perth's certified green buildings, on the other hand, share many things with T3, which is certified green by Singapore's Building & Construction Authority for its energy and water savings.[3] For example, the new low-rise office building at 2 Victoria Avenue in Perth's CBD appears more open, fragmented and transparent than the buildings around it. This building has been certified by the Green Building Council of Australia industry association for its construction management and commissioning processes, indoor environmental quality, energy- and water-saving systems, support of public and small-vehicle transport, appropriate land use and emissions management.[4] Through a checklist process, the developer demonstrated that its glass building on Victoria Avenue satisfied enough of the council's criteria to be green.

Buildings are important sites for negotiating society's responses to ecological crisis, partly because they can be shown to account for a third of the world's energy-related carbon-dioxide emissions.[5] The building industry wants to keep building – so sophisticated actors in the industry have focused their attention on the development of green buildings as a relevant solution in the age of ecological crisis. Green buildings are positioned as outperforming standard buildings in mitigating anthropogenic climate change[6] and other ecological threats. Green buildings and their designs are connoted by rating symbols such as 'Green Star' in Australia,[7] which are generally distributed through national associations of representatives from industry, government and academia. The reliability of these symbols is then determined in the fields of marketing and public relations.[8] The World Green Building Council (WorldGBC) has established itself as the peak international actor influencing professional discussions about building in the age of ecological crisis. Within the first decade of its establishment, the WorldGBC's membership had grown to include more than eighty national green-building councils.[9] These national councils receive guidance from the world council on promoting green-building markets and establishing national certification systems. A national system's green-building standards are negotiated by council members representing the interests of their organisations – typically in property development, architecture, engineering and manufacturing – while promoting the industry of green building within the local governmental context.[10] These certification systems help to stabilise the meaning of 'green building' for the work of building professionals, investors, tenants, bureaucrats, politicians and journalists. However, the meanings of each green-building project are still up for negotiation within the cultural milieu of its construction site. This can be a lengthy process in which a property developer sets out to achieve corporate objectives through negotiations with investors, tenants, architects, engineers, contractors, certification agencies and planning authorities, as well as with the communities around the building site. If negotiation goes well for a developer, its green built environment will satisfy core corporate objectives as well as its target market's sense of appropriate measures for dealing with ecological threats. Within this negotiation, developers – like other corporations – tend to position themselves as moral actors in order to shape public perception of their products. This is done through a public-relations strategy of appearing 'to be disclosing more while actually enclosing on what is publicized'.[11] However, developers must share the field of public relations with government, industry associations, news organisations, experts, environmental activists and citizen groups which demonstrate relevancy and organisation while promoting their particular interests.

Property developers have a more problematic field than manufacturers of other products (such as appliances) because their construction sites are also their consumption sites. As soon as construction works begin it is difficult to hide the fact that the local environment is being disturbed in some way, and that emissions are being released. The developer's product can only be viewed as green at sufficient spatial and temporal distance from the construction site. Seeing a building's marketing materials on the other side of Australia, it seems as though no environmental damage is being done in producing the product. After the building has been built, one no longer sees the construction or pre-construction environment. However green a building may look from a distant time or place, local immediate environmental concerns about it persist. The building industry deals with the politics of this environmental proximity problem by appealing to society's recognition of future global ecological crisis. Facing up to this crisis can be represented as an argument for the globally-coordinated manufacture of new buildings equipped with technologies for mitigating the crisis: 'Since our establishment in 2002, we have been working closely with councils to promote local green building actions and address global issues such as climate change,' says the WorldGBC.[12] By promoting the green-building market globally, the WorldGBC works 'to ensure that green buildings are a part of any comprehensive strategy to deliver carbon-emission reductions'.[13] So long as green buildings are seen to mitigate climate change, the climate-change threat mitigates resistance to green buildings; or so it seems.

The stakes are high, with calls for 'radical departures from normal planning- and decision-making processes' in the production of eco-cities.[14] These radical departures include a global shift towards expert groups and invited community participation in determining urban planning policy, away from the antagonistic struggles of engaged publics and municipal institutions. Although the language around eco-cities and green buildings may seem new, there is nothing new about attempting to limit policy making in urban planning to the domain of engineers and other experts guided by vision-oriented reformist thinking.

More than a century ago, Ebenezer Howard hoped to achieve an ideal, stable society through the development of green-field city utopias that would be managed by powerful corporations responsive to rent-paying tenant voters rather than to existing municipalities.[15] These Garden Cities would adopt pollution- and sprawl-reducing technologies, as well as closed loop systems for turning sewage into fertilizer for local food production. Howard's treatise, originally published in 1898 as '*Tomorrow: a Peaceful Path to Real Reform*',[16] called for city planning by technocrats:

> It will no doubt be the work of many minds – the minds
> of engineers, of architects and surveyors, of landscape
> gardeners and electricians. But it is essential, as we have

said, that there should be unity of design and purpose…
Garden City is not only planned, but it is planned with a
view to the very latest of modern requirements…[17]

Similar language can be found in very recent materials promoting big green-building projects and eco-cities around the
world. Yet, what is often missed is that the objective of Howard's
influential treatise was the implementation of a peaceful method of
social reform, as stated clearly in the original title. This emphasis
has been lost partly because later editions of his book appeared
with a modified title, '*Garden Cities of To-morrow*';[18] suggesting that
Howard's goal was to reform urban planning to create a spatial
utopia. This subtle change in stated objectives may have helped
Howard's text to seem new, but its original stated objective has
been traced back through time to Thomas More's artificially
created island of Utopia.[19] More suggested that a radically different
society could occur in a constructed space where its people were
disconnected from existing places. This ideal space of no place,
according to More, was a man-made island off the mainland
coast. In this space of no place, radical social reform could occur.
Five hundred years later, renderings of More's Utopia[20] bear an
uncanny resemblance to those of North Port Quay.

In early 2009, the North Port Quay consortium called on
Fremantle's citizens to support its plan 'to build a sustainable new
community' at its potentially world-leading 'carbon-neutral urban
development' off the coast.[21] This island of ecological modernisation would include applied technologies from around the world:
to run homes on locally generated renewable energy; to use solar
power for large-scale housing through a smart electricity grid; to
collect and desalinate water locally using wave power; and to use
the rock-wall construction methods that apparently worked in San

Francisco Bay, at Hong Kong airport and Kansai airport Japan. The list of technologies was long and fashionable. North Port Quay would aim 'to combine all these innovations to build a sustainable new community'.[22] North Port Quay's advertising suggested that these innovations had worked in overseas projects, though it was impossible to confirm this claim without considerable research. Pictures of these innovations, which appeared in the company's advertising, worked to create associations for the reader between North Port Quay and other green building projects, diverting attention away from problems with any single environmental claim on behalf of the project. Also, this list of green-building symbols was presented with an ideological dilemma:[23] whether the Fremantle reader was for or against doing things sustainably. The consortium called on readers to take a stand on this dilemma by supporting North Port Quay in the kind of populist terminology typically employed by the Fremantle Football Club: 'C'mon Freo, let's put it all together and lead the world'.[24] Local supporters envisaged the project as a must-see destination for tourists of ecological modernisation: 'North Port Quay to our north will be a must-see vibrant destination attracting visitors by conceptual boldness, varied architecture and advanced environmental performance,' wrote John Bird.[25] Supporters focused on North Port Quay's future environmental performance, often in terms of an implied global competition for sustainability and attention.

Yet representations of North Port Quay as a green built environment defied an internal logic typically found in institutional discourses of green building. This logic involved supporters of a green building representing a particular ecological threat along with a scientifically supported argument that the building's long-term operational performance could mitigate this threat. Through this logic, a green building may suggest an ecological threat and its solution as well as the moral authority of its developer in taking action to mitigate that particular ecological threat. Typically, a green building mitigates climate change through its expected superior operational performance, leading to lower carbon emissions over the building lifecycle. Yet, attempts to make this argument work for North Port Quay were continually disrupted by more immediate concerns about the level of carbon emissions from such an extensive reclamation project. If climate change is already upon us, then why aggravate it further? Professor Newman tried valiantly to keep the ecological crisis real but in the future: the 'carbon-constrained future'.[26] He argued that 'the importance of innovative experiments in sustainability is much too critical for such dialogue [rejecting sustainability claims]. Perth has an opportunity to become a global leader due to this visionary concept. I hope I can help to see this happen.'[27]

One of the problems that Newman had to contest was that North Port Quay's futuristic imagery didn't match the kind of sustainability that many people had come to expect in Fremantle. Locals were looking to some kind of bottom-up, organic version of sustainability.[28] Generally, they were worried about pollution, rising sea levels, overpopulation and resource limits. Many were residents in Fremantle out of nostalgia or to take a break from the transformative and competitive rigours of global capitalism – when the radical North Port Quay development came along to contest someone's idea of a race to be the 'world's first carbon-free development'.[29] Powerboats and motorcars as well as gluttony and competition appeared in the project's initial public imagery. These images had little in common with the familiar representations of sustainability in the local press, such as the mayor and future mayor promoting cycling and bicycle sharing.

Newman also had to contend with concerns about the North Port Quay island development's location. This utopian island would mess with people's memories of a beloved beach. It was too close and its construction too obviously destructive to be green, at least in the political constituency of its regulators.

Professor Newman was forced to defend his position and his reputation from the outset. 'I have an arrangement with NPQ,' he said, 'to establish a sustainability plan based on a series of expert inputs which I will coordinate and will set out the main concepts in the plan'.[30] He said that this would be 'followed by some detailed work where my Curtin University Sustainability Policy (CUSP) Institute will be provided with research scholarships. I am not paid personally for this work'.[31]

North Port Quay's project manager, Chris Carman, tried to come to Newman's aid on several occasions in the local press. As his team prepared to register their design for accreditation with the Green Building Council of Australia for a rating assessment, he told the *Fremantle Herald*: 'Our concept aims to address the climate change on a scale never before contemplated.'[32]

Notes

1   *Fremantle Gazette*, 10 February 2009, pp. 24–5.
2   E. Howard, *Garden Cities of To-morrow*, Faber and Faber, London, 1946, p. 77.
3   *Green Mark for Buildings Award*, Building Construction Authority, Singapore, viewed 8 April 2014, <http://www.bca.gov.sg/greenmark/others/gm2010.pdf>.
4   Green Star Project Directory, Green Building Council Australia, Sydney, viewed 8 April 2014, <http://www.gbca.org.au/project-directory.asp#809>.
5   S. Koeppel & D. Ürge-Vorsatz, *Assessment of Policy Instruments for Reducing Greenhouse Gas Emissions from Buildings*, United Nations Environment Programme and Central European University, Budapest, 2007.
6   J. Miller, *Tackling Global Climate Change: Meeting Local Priorities*, World Green Building Council, Toronto, 2010.

7   *Green star*, Green Building Council Australia, Sydney, viewed 11 May 2009, <http://www.gbca.org.au/green-star/>.

8   R. Madew, *Directors' Report*, Green Building Council Australia, Sydney, 2008, pp. 3–13.

9   *What are GBCs?*, World Green Building Council, Toronto, viewed 3 August 2011, <http://www.worldgbc.org/site2/index.php?cID=126>.

10 T. Kerr, 'Sustainability discourse and the green building', Honours thesis, Curtin University, 2008, p. 60.

11 R.V. Ericson, P. M. Baranek & J. B. L Chan, *Negotiating Control: A Study of News Sources,* Open University Press, Milton Keynes, 1989, p. 383.

12 *About WorldGBC*, World Green Building Council, Toronto, viewed 8 April 2014, <http://www.worldgbc.org/worldgbc/about/>.

13 Ibid.

14 J. R. Kenworthy, 'The eco-city: ten key transport and planning dimensions for sustainable city development', *Environment and Urbanization*, vol. 18, no. 1, 2006, p. 82.

15 E. Howard, *Garden Cities of To-morrow*, Faber and Faber, London, 1946, pp. 50–92.

16 Preface by F. J. Osborn in Howard, *Garden Cities of To-morrow*, p. 9.

17 Howard, *Garden Cities of To-morrow*, pp. 76–7.

18 Preface by Osborn in Howard, *Garden Cities of To-morrow*, p. 9.

19 D. Harvey, *Spaces of Hope*, Edinburgh University Press, Edinburgh, 2000, pp. 159–73.

20 T. More, 'Utopia' in S. Bruce (ed), *Three Early Modern Utopias: Thomas More: Utopia / Francis Bacon: New Atlantis / Henry Neville: The Isle of Pines*, Oxford University Press, Oxford, 1999. pp. 1–148.

21 *Fremantle Gazette*, 10 February 2009, pp. 24–5.

22 Ibid.

23 L. Chouliaraki, 'Mediation, text and action', in V. K. Bhatia, J. Flowerdew & R. H. Jones (eds), *Advances in Discourse Studies,* Routledge, London, 2008, pp. 211–27.

24 *Fremantle Gazette*, 10 February 2009, pp. 24–5.

25 *Fremantle Herald*, 29 November 2008, p. 5.

26 *Fremantle Herald*, 7 June 2008, p. 2.

27 Ibid.

28 *Fremantle Herald*, 28 June 2008, p. 5.

29 *Fremantle Herald*, 14 June 2008, p. 7.

30 *Fremantle Herald*, 7 June 2008, p. 2.

31 Ibid.

32 *Fremantle Herald*, 20 September 2008, p. 2.

GREENWASH

Representation of North Port Quay in *Fremantle Herald*

'*North Port Quay has the potential to be the most sustainable residential, marina, recreational, tourism development in the world.*'[1]

North Port Quay

Unlike Harry Potter's cloak of invisibility,[2] North Port Quay's cloak of sustainability was seen to fool very few characters in its story – which was being told in local newspapers. This disbelief was most pronounced in letters and opinion pieces by people with subject authority through association with academic research institutions.

Curtin University's Emeritus Professor, David Hawks – an experienced researcher of drug and alcohol addiction – posed an immediate challenge to North Port Quay and its principal sustainability advocate. Hawks asked Professor Newman to make all his calculations publicly available in support of the claim that North Port Quay would 'be the first carbon-neutral development in Australia'.[3] Has Newman 'worked out the number of years it will need to repay the grid for its profligate expenditure of energy in its construction?' He suggested that building on that scale over the sea and 'the complexity of its sewerage and other disposal networks will result in an expenditure of energy which will make any positive return of energy light years away.' Hawks' reproach didn't stop there: 'just how sustainable are buildings exposed to the corrosive and unpredictable environment of the sea? Surely to build over the sea, given our spacious land, is a crime against nature?'[4] A couple of months after the project's launch, Hawks turned his attention to the ethical problem of a university professor making public scientific claims supporting North Port Quay. The *Fremantle Herald* published Hawks' 'Carbonated' letter below a cartoon of four executives around a meeting table, saying: 'I don't know why they don't believe we're green minded...we even smoke our cigars OUTSIDE the board room.'[5] Then three months after the launch, the *Herald* published an op-ed article by Hawks, which highlighted the newspaper's 'indulgence in allowing Peter Newman a two-page spread to advertise his sustainability credentials'.[6] Hawks suggested the *Herald* had provided too much space for Peter Newman, acting as 'chief marketing agent', 'to add a green tinge' to North Port Quay. In undermining publicity attempts to make NPQ seem green, Hawks asked a series of questions starting with: 'When, after the construction costs in terms of carbon emissions are added up, will it become carbon neutral?... How many of the development's 2,000 boats will be diesel or petrol driven?' Hawks problematised the objectivity of environmental claims made in support of North Port Quay by asking: 'Who has determined that the seabed is degraded and what does degraded mean?' Hawks then turned his attention to something he knew a lot about: the problem of ethical relations between university researchers and commercial organisations. Hawks asked what percentage of Curtin University's Sustainability Policy (CUSP) Institute's income was derived from North Port Quay. He asked why wasn't the involvement of this institute, directed by Newman, 'processed through Curtin University's normal ethical procedures?'[7] Hawks suggested that Newman's association with the project was misguided if not self-serving, even if the funds went directly into much-needed scholarships. Debate within the academy over North Port Quay burst into the public sphere in mid-September 2008; local academics were reportedly turning on Professor Newman over his support for North Port Quay and his suggestion that Fremantle Council's planning authority should be over-ridden by state government:

> At a sustainability forum attended by a swag of boffins last week Murdoch Uni lecturer Adam McHugh challenged the prof to prove he'd done his homework on claims NPQ would be carbon neutral.

"He said there was no methodology. He admitted it in front of the crowd and went on to try to defend it saying 'it's just a dream'," Mr McHugh said.

But Prof Newman later accused his former protégé of not listening as he described the commonwealth government's Greenhouse Friendly methodology, which measures completed development – not carbon used in construction.

"[Adam] obviously wasn't listening, but he never listens," Prof Newman fired back.

Fremantle Society president Ian Alexander, a Curtin Uni town planning adjunct professor, wasn't listening either.

"[Peter Newman] said no model was done it was just 'aspirational'," Dr Alexander said.[8]

Associate Professor Brad Pettitt of Murdoch University's sustainability department joined the debate, maintaining that little had changed in North Port Quay's revised plan for the new government except for the lowering of a seawall which 'made a mockery of claims it was required to protect the islands from rising sea levels'.[9] Pettitt, who was also a Fremantle councillor, disrupted the environmental case for North Port Quay by focusing on associations between carbon control, climate change and rising sea levels. 'It must mean that the experts decided that climate change was going to be less severe than we thought about three months ago,' Pettitt said sarcastically.[10] Criticism also came from the University of Western Australia, with Landscape Architecture Professor Richard Weller calling the North Port Quay reclamation project an 'aesthetically questionable...sprawl towards Rottnest'.[11]

Peter Newman tried to defend the project and his credibility through letters to the Fremantle press. As CUSP's Professor of Sustainability, Newman argued his institute was not established with money from big business like North Port Quay, rather it was set up to support postgraduate research and teaching at Curtin University: 'Our main activities so far have been teaching a Masters in Sustainability Studies, and research in fields such as climate change and energy policies'.[12] The institute's research also covered 'coastal sustainability, deliberative democracy and governance, ecotourism, migration and diaspora, new technologies, sense of place, sustainability economics, sustainability education, sustainable transportation, urban and regional sustainability'.[13] Newman tried to defend his call for a state development authority to handle local planning issues by saying that such a body would not 'mean the end of local democracy'. Yet, facing mounting criticism for his support of North Port Quay and a shift away from municipal planning, Newman offered to withdraw temporarily from the public sphere.[14] Critics would not let Newman take leave so easily. Sandy Boulter, the coordinator of SpeakOutWA!, argued that the community would be less suspicious of Newman's support for a Fremantle regional-development authority if he also supported the right of legal appeal against unlawful or unmeritorious development approvals which would give 'our poor local government town planners a break from the developer tactics they often suffer in the absence of such rights'.[15] Meanwhile, local residents demanded answers to the questions posed by academics. Joe Dortch wanted Newman to say 'how many tonnes of rock and concrete' would be needed for North Port Quay given that Newman 'or his clients' should know since they promised the development would be 'sustainable and carbon-neutral'.[16] By his calculations and references, Dortch said it would take about 50 million tonnes of rocks and sand and 5 million tonnes of concrete to reclaim the North Port Quay site and build the seawall, generating more than 1.5 million tonnes of carbon-dioxide equivalent. Dortch said the sustainability claims were nonsense because producing North Port Quay's construction materials alone 'could emit double the CO_2 saved annually by phasing out wasteful incandescent light bulbs across Australia, as recently legislated, or by taking half a million cars off the road'. The consortium seemed to have no plan to offset its emissions from construction infill, according to Dortch: 'It should, because it doesn't need to be in the ocean…So, please, NPQ tell us how construction will be sustainable'.[17]

Professor Newman was accused of being ignorant, cynical and partial in defining progress: 'To create mindlessly ugly, expansive developments in the name of progress is a misnomer and cynical,'[18] said Beck Wilson in Beaconsfield, overlooking Fremantle. She said views of progress needed 'to be re-quantified to include the things that are vital to positive social and environmental outcomes. Destruction of the environment jeopardises our very survival and is therefore unsustainable…Continued expansion without regard for people and their need to live in clean, safe, positive environ-ments is also not sustainable.' Newman was not speaking 'for our kids', said Wilson.[19] Nor was he speaking for the thousands who turned out in January that year to save Fremantle's beaches from development at sea, said Save Freo Beaches Alliance's convenor Michael Martin.[20] He announced that the alliance's members were getting ready to support an opposition group to North Port Quay because the change in government had opened the pos-sibility of it proceeding. Martin, a clean-cut bureaucrat, focused on North Port Quay's long-term cost to taxpayers due to storm flooding at high tides when the sea levels rose 'from one metre to a ghastly four metres':

The risk for future generations of tax payers is that the threat from long-term sea-level rise is being minimised in the interest of short-term profits.

Will the developers be around in 50 years and willing to pick up the tab for additional and substantial capital works to protect assets threatened with inundations? I think not!

The tax payer will be in line to pay at the very time that such inundation is occurring all along our coast and rivers.[21]

You didn't have to be an academic to see that North Port Quay was unsustainable, said Martin, who was also a member of the Greens party. Construction emissions should be counted before 'setting down to the detail of how the buildings will be powered and people transported'. The new government should constrain this greed-fuelled nonsense, he said. 'Residential development immediately on the coast or on land reclaimed from the sea-bed is not only unsustainable, it is manifestly stupid,' said the seasoned campaigner. 'The need to plan for sea-level rise, pull back from the coast and impose some limits to greed is screaming at us,' said Martin: 'But will our new state government listen?'[22] Apparently the government was listening. By late September, it was becoming clear that the Liberal government would not support North Port Quay. Although the new planning minister, John Day, was pushing for some kind of marina development at Rous Head, he said his leader would not tolerate the 345-hectare plan.[23] Indeed, Premier Barnett had called the consortium arrogant for thinking it could buy the ocean bed.

Not only was the new government's leadership against the project and its chief environmental spokesperson under pressure for claiming 'a miraculous carbon-free terra-formation',[24] North Port Quay's design would not meet the accreditation criteria of Australia's peak organisation for green building. The Green Building Council of Australia had recently adopted a policy that made coastal reclamation projects ineligible for its Green Star rating. Ian Scott wrote in the *Herald* that the 'Green Building Council of Australia will not even consider offices, houses or hotels built on new sea infill as being appropriate in terms of environmental acceptability.'[25] Scott, who became an accredited professional of the Green Building Council, asked: 'where to now guys with your unassessable North Port Quay?'[26]

But North Port Quay's backers had a bigger problem with their sustainability claims. In late 2008, a complaint was lodged with the Australian Competition and Consumer Commission (ACCC) about the project's publicity. The complaint came to light when the consortium's chief, Greg Poland, described it as a 'desperate and shameful' abuse of the law.[27] Although the ACCC would not confirm that an investigation was underway, Poland's comments in the *Herald* confirmed it for readers: 'Unnamed complainants have objected to statements that [NPQ] would be the world's first carbon-free development'.[28] Against the backdrop of this ACCC investigation, it was suggested that 'NPQ sustainability consultant, Professor Peter Newman' and 'Murdoch sustainability expert Brad Pettitt' were at loggerheads over the project.[29] Newman was seen to suggest that project opponents were ignorant of the latest technological advances while Pettitt called on the consortium to make supporting evidence available for scrutiny. The ACCC would eventually find that North Port Quay had overstated its green credentials, and that it should 'tone down its carbon-neutral claims' or face a $1.2 million fine.[30] Brad Pettitt's credibility as an Associate Professor of Sustainability would be assured in the local community, helping him along the road to becoming Fremantle's next mayor. 'The claims for carbon neutrality or the new term they are using which is carbon free, I think,' he said with a shrug, 'are claims they provide no evidence for and there is no sense that they can be justified.'[31]

Public-relations attempts to position North Port Quay as 'a world-leading example of sustainable development'[32] were failing because ecological threats suggested in the PR narrative were not complemented by solutions to these threats. In other words, North Port Quay's publicity lacked the type of threat–solution narrative that normally suggested green built environment: For a building project to be legitimised by an ecological threat it must seem like a solution to this threat. The problem facing PR professionals is that a suggested ecological threat can be read in many ways due to the diversity of experiences of members of their target audiences. The dominance of North Port Quay's seawall in public imagery suggested rising sea levels, aggravated by immediate carbon emissions. It did not represent a solution to the 'carbon-constrained future'[33] described by Peter Newman. While publicists could try to influence readings of threats, they could not control them. Distant, future ecological problems were again being over-ridden by concerns over more-immediate threats to the local environment.

The New Year's editions of *Fremantle Herald* continued to undermine North Port Quay's sustainability claims. The newspaper published its 'www.bigseabucks' cartoon again, representing the project as a 'wonderful concept in money-making with eco-aspects tacked on to get locals on side'.[34] It also republished a by-now familiar rendering of North Port Quay's seawall with a statement that 'views of Rottnest would be obliterated'.[35] Recalling major media events of 2008, North Port Quay's launch was reduced to alien invasion: 'It's D-Day as developers continue their assault on our beaches, with the mother of all developments, the $10 billion North Port Quay'.[36] Not afraid to blow its own trumpet, the *Herald* reminded readers that debate over the project had almost been over-shadowed by its 'cheeky reference to project consultant Peter Newman as a sustainability gun-for-hire'. The newspaper published a photograph of Peter Newman at the Carriage Café in the park by the Esplanade with the cafe's owner Kel Smith and former premier Peter Dowding. In the pleasant shade of Norfolk Island pines, the white-haired Newman smiles and appears relaxed in a turtleneck and sports coat with his little white long-haired dog stretching over his lap. Although Newman seemed most at ease helping to defend this popular cafe against removal under a proposed master plan for the park, the newspaper wouldn't let him return to the fold of the people. It captioned the photograph: 'Peter Newman hangs out with his lapdog (that's the one with the white mane, big teeth...oh, you know what we mean)'.[37] The new year heralded trouble for Newman as North Port Quay came 'under more fire',[38] this time from the grandson of the mid-twentieth-century union activist Paddy Troy – a man embedded in Fremantle's historical narrative: The wooden benches Paddy Troy installed for impoverished dockworkers, who used to sit waiting opposite what was then Fremantle's Trades Hall, are still highly visible under the Esplanade Hotel verandah. Paddy's grandson, Professor Patrick Troy of the Australian National University, weighed into the academics' argument over the environmental meaning of North Port Quay, saying that Newman had lost sight of research showing that high-rise development did more environmental harm than good. 'The energy cost of the construction and the building materials alone are unsustainable,' he said.[39] Professor Troy said the project's 'self-appointed experts' had elevated themselves 'beyond review or reproach'.[40] Retired professor David Hawks supported Troy's statement, and described as inadequate Newman's response to criticism of his carbon-free claim: 'To observe that one "can aspire to be carbon-free overnight" hardly seems an adequate response,' Hawks said. At least Professor Troy 'cannot be dismissed as "an objector unaware of rapidly emerging technologies"'.[41] Even by April 2009, Hawks maintained that North Port Quay was still to define what it meant by carbon neutrality, 'let alone demonstrate it when taking into account the energy costs of the project's construction'.[42] David Hawks called the project an inspired act of theft, representing 'a morally and ecologically indefensible sequestration of a public asset, the sea'.[43] North Port Quay was a transgression in the common sense of Fremantle.

Notes

1   *Fremantle Gazette,* 10 June 2008, p. 15.
2   J. K. Rowling, *Harry Potter and the Philosopher's Stone,* Bloomsbury, London, 1997.
3   *Fremantle Herald,* 7 June 2008, p. 4.
4   Ibid.
5   *Fremantle Herald,* 2 August 2008, p. 4.
6   *Fremantle Herald,* 13 September 2008, p. 3.
7   Ibid.
8   Ibid., p. 7.
9   *Fremantle Herald,* 20 September 2008, p. 2.
10 Ibid.
11 *Fremantle Herald,* 20 September 2008, p. 27.
12 Ibid., p. 6.
13 Ibid.
14 Ibid.
15 Ibid.
16 Ibid.
17 Ibid.
18 *Fremantle Herald,* 27 September 2008, p. 4.

19   Ibid.

20   Ibid., p. 5.

21   Ibid.

22   Ibid.

23   *Fremantle Herald*, 27 September 2008, p. 1.

24   *Fremantle Herald*, 4 October 2008, p. 16.

25   *Fremantle Herald*, 30 August 2008, p. 4.

26   Ibid.

27   *Fremantle Herald*, 20 December 2008, p. 3.

28   Ibid.

29   Ibid.

30   *Fremantle Herald*, 9 May 2009, p. 1.

31   'Fremantle quay issue', ABC News WA, Perth, 9 May 2009.

32   *Fremantle Gazette*, 10 June 2008, p. 15.

33   *Fremantle Herald*, 7 June 2008, p. 2.

34   *Fremantle Herald*, 27 December 2008, p. 14.

35   Ibid., p. 16.

36   Ibid.

37   *Fremantle Herald*, 3 January 2009, p. 16.

38   *Fremantle Herald*, 10 January 2009, p. 14.

39   *Fremantle Herald*, 11 October 2008, p. 2.

40   *Fremantle Herald*, 10 January 2009, p. 14.

41   *Fremantle Herald*, 17 January 2009, p. 4.

42   *Fremantle Herald*, 25 April 2009, p. 35.

43   Ibid.

IMAGINING FREMANTLE

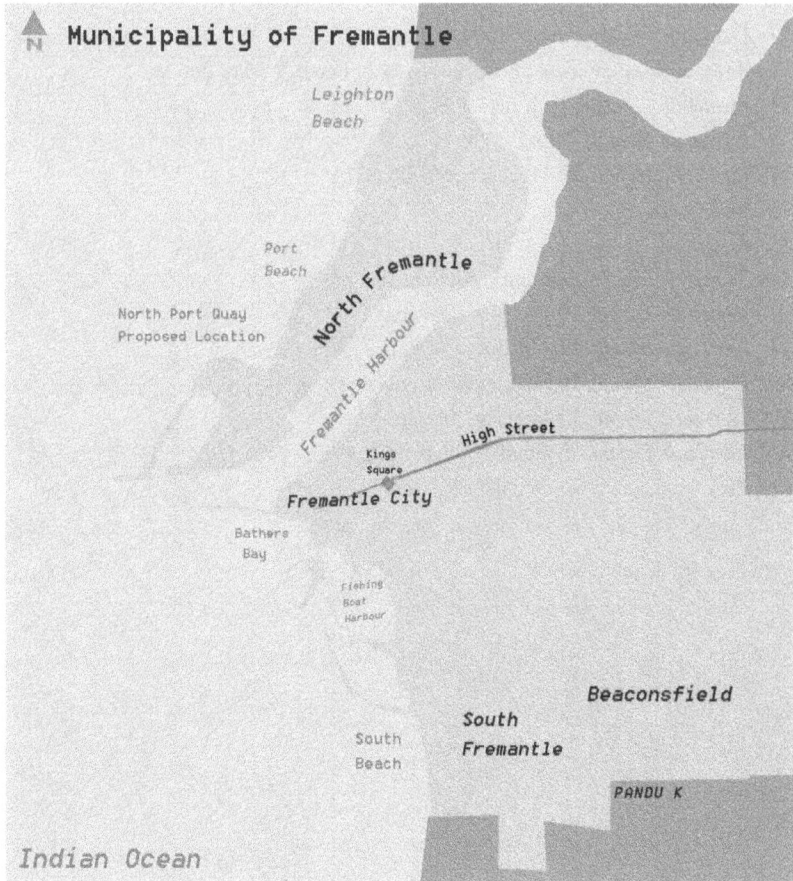

Imagined by Pandu Kerr

Fre-o way to go, hit 'em real hard and send them below.[1]
Club song lyrics, Fremantle Dockers Football Club

Fremantle meets the three main criteria of being an imagined community, according to the seminal work of Benedict Anderson: the community's population mostly don't know each other as individuals; the community has a boundary beyond which are other communities; and the community conceives a 'deep horizontal comradeship' for itself.[2] Seeing Fremantle through Anderson's criteria provides insight into public reaction to North Port Quay.

Like all larger-than-village habitations, people in Fremantle imagine they know their community while not actually knowing everyone in it as individuals, meeting Anderson's first criterion. Long-serving Fremantle councillor Les Lauder appeared confident in his knowledge of Fremantle community, whether he was in the council chamber arguing that North Port Quay is 'just not what Fremantle wants'[3] or in the press claiming that 'Fremantle is crying out for leadership'.[4] Yet, knowledge of community relies on such public expressions as it is impossible to know what all its members privately want. Almost 5,000 people a year were moving into the Fremantle local-government area before the launch of North Port Quay, and half of these people were coming from places outside of Western Australia.[5] Indeed, about a third of Fremantle's 25,000 residents were born overseas. Once inside the Fremantle local-government area, most people live in distinct houses, typically with a small garden. Less than a third of residents inhabit a semi-detached house, terrace house or apartment.[6] Publicly imagining this heterogeneous mobile population as a stable community with collective wants is a key function of local media and government, as seen in the work of a very determined Councillor Lauder.

Before Fremantle was constructed as an imagined community and physical town with a distinct boundary, Walyalup was an important place for crossing what were then sandbars between the heads of what is commonly known today as the 'Swan River'. The next major crossing was a long walk upstream to Matagarup, the sacred Aboriginal gathering place at what is now commonly known as Heirisson Island, near Perth's central business district.[7] After Fremantle's arrival, Walyalup was removed from public conversation – as was the sandbar crossing, pulled from the mouth of the Swan River. Colonists established Fremantle as a trade gateway from where people would travel, initially by river boat, to Perth, the administrative capital of Western Australia. The first shipload of private settlers to arrive in Fremantle moved to the beach,[8] accommodating themselves there in tents while waiting for a land-allotment survey of Nyoongar *boodja* to be drafted by John Roe. The Aboriginal people's country was mapped as land allotments on paper, which were occupied rapidly for free by British private investors; imminent colonial violence threatened anyone challenging their occupation. Property development was integral to this particular British invasion, and its success was largely assured once the private investors had moved inland from the beach into houses they and their servants built on the allotments. Under pressure of new arrivals, Roe quickly produced a survey of allotments in Fremantle, and this grid-like town plan can be seen largely intact today in the west end of Fremantle. Trade in these free allotments emerged almost immediately with the first sale of an allotment recorded in late 1829.[9] As the Western Australia colony developed, Fremantle grew as its distribution centre. The colony's first newspaper was set up there in 1830 as was its first printing press.[10] However, the difficulty of getting large ships into and out of its port retarded Fremantle's growth until dredging and construction works, headed by Charles O'Connor, radically altered the harbour by the turn of the twentieth century.

Thereafter, the town's population increased rapidly and in 1929 Fremantle was proclaimed a city.[11] The physical urban boundaries of Perth and Fremantle merged in the second half of the twentieth century, although Fremantle remained distinguishable on maps and in popular representation of Fremantle community. The municipality's *Our Place* cultural plan[12] described Fremantle's evolving urban identity as a unique mix, with distinct features valued by residents and visitors alike:

> Its history as a meeting place for Aboriginal people pre-European settlement; its physical location at the mouth of the Swan River; its history as the Western Gateway to Australia and the first point of arrival for many immigrants; its importance as a working harbour and fishing centre; its significant heritage buildings; its strong labour history; its arts, cultural and sporting activities; and its community spirit all shape Fremantle's identity.[13]

Our Place imagined Fremantle as an inclusive community that transcended race and social class, advocating that this 'sense of community' be strengthened through the promotion of 'the distinctive local identity of Fremantle'.[14] According to the plan, the municipality should do more to clearly distinguish Fremantle from other communities, and this work should be done with the river and ocean providing orientation and sense of identity for the imagined community. While this orientation seemed clear, the city's cultural planners had to address concerns articulated within the community that a cultural program focusing too narrowly on Fremantle's maritime heritage and early, colonial built environment risked turning the city into a theme park:

There is community concern that the definition of heritage is too limited and that there is at times a nostalgic view of what is 'good'. There is limited recognition of traditions outside 19th-Century English heritage. Interpretation of historical sites is underdeveloped and there is insufficient documentation of recent history.[15]

Cultural scientist John Hartley argued that Fremantle could not be authenticated by its origins or current built environment because 'Fremantling' had turned the place into a pleasurama, 'reality into sideshow, and symbolic identity into an import/export commodity'.[16] When 2,000 journalists arrived there to produce the America's Cup media spectacle in late 1986 to early 1987, the Fremantle backdrop for the yacht race revealed its own strategic purpose in not only imagining Fremantle but also imagining Western Australia and Australia:[17]

> However, the visit of Bob Hawke, the genial prime minister of Australia, strolling the sunny streets of the Fremantle set after officially unfurling yet another gigantic Australian flag over the Roundhouse, WA's oldest building and first prison, suggests that the higher levels of government, at least, understand only too well the need to unify people into an imagined community of citizens who can be mobilized to see themselves as free to choose in the name not of ideology but of euphoria.[18]

Hartley suggested that people made more sense of democracy as a competition for spectators than as a practice for citizens. However, this sense of spectatorship maintained by media organisations across space may be disrupted on the ground in Fremantle where democracy can be sensed as something much more intimate in the mosaic of a port town. The mosaic performance of Fremantle – bolstered by municipal support for street art – enables locals and tourists to feel at home, or at least part of the Fremantle theatre, where a sense of comradeship can be felt by the cast. It seems as though anyone can become an actor there among the ambiguous props on the Fremantle stage. Australia's cultural giants, the local front-men of major shifts in twentieth-century thinking, such as wartime prime minister John Curtin and legendary Bon Scott of AC/DC, appear in Fremantle as comic statues. These Smurf-like twenty-first-century reproductions make any homage to Curtin and Scott in Fremantle highly ambiguous. There appears to be something for everyone in this place, catering to consumers and offering relief from suburban Perth – which never quite became a post-industrial city. Perth remains the administrative gateway for exploiting Western Australia's minerals and forests in an enduring colonial act of arriving, seizing, converting and selling natural resources that were apparently underexploited by other people. These acts began in Fremantle, but the industries involved in this production have been pushed out of Fremantle's centre to its fringes over the last century.[19] The town centre has been transformed into a post-industrial hub centred on cultural artefacts and services. It appears to support forms of resistance, but just within the horizon of an Australian imagining, which in recent decades has become increasingly intolerant of ideas, people and institutions that could challenge the power of neo-liberal elites, particularly owners of production.[20] In its centre, Fremantle's one-time jails have become tourist attractions, its lunatic asylum an arts centre, and its trades hall a Buddhist restaurant. Fremantle's main upmarket corporate hotel is decorated with the benches for day workers donated by communist leader Paddy Troy in mid-last century. The popular

Esplanade Park with magnificent not-quite-native trees was a beach last century. Nearby, public grants have reproduced imaginings of late-nineteenth-century merchant society in the West End of Fremantle; and within many of these low-rise buildings the 25-year-old Notre Dame University looks like it has been around for 125 years. At least in this part of Fremantle, amid all this simulacra, the only things worth defending as authentic appear to be the stage itself and fellow actors. The backdrop of this stage is the port and the theatre seems at risk without it, which is why *Our Place* emphasised that a working port was integral to Fremantle's cultural value.[21] This cultural plan also called for the maintenance of the depth and diversity of Fremantle's built and natural environment because such heritage was essential in enabling diverse Fremantle narratives. The Portuguese, Italian and other European migrants who settled there, as well as the artists and people on the economic margins who lived there when it was still cheap enough to do so, all contributed in some way to the diversity of these narratives. Without this polyphony of voices – required for contemporary creative production[22] – the Fremantle theatre risks collapsing into mundane suburban Perth and losing its boundary once and for all. This community at Fremantle's boundary satisfies Anderson's second criterion.

The third criterion for an imagined community, a sense of egalitarian comradeship, can be identified in the successful reworking of community identity around the Fremantle Football Club (FFC). The corporation behind the FFC, launched in 1994, successfully exploited the Fremantle stage to build a large supporter base and revenue stream, despite the club's home ground being Subiaco and its original player affiliation with Claremont – suburbs identified with Perth rather than Fremantle.[23] In its first season the club's players ran onto the oval through an inflatable container ship rather than a traditional banner, which lead to the club's Rock and Anchor Ceremony before home games.[24] Fremantle was the second Australian Football League club to be licensed for Western Australia after the West Coast Eagles, which represented a state-wide supporter base. The club looked for several points of differentiation from the Eagles in its own representation, class interest being key as argued in the PhD thesis of Gervase Haimes:

> ...the main differentiation instigated by FFC was the concept of FFC as a community club and it incorporated the moniker, "The people's Club", into its formal company documentation such as letterheads and fax cover sheets. This differentiation was attempted to show up the West Coast Eagles as being from the rich part of town with big corporate sponsorship as its support (infamously drinking chardonnay) whilst FFC was a humble club supported by the common man with a "blue collar" background thus reinforcing the theme that the club was creating for itself as a working man's club from a working class port city. The indication of both clubs' research were that these differences were entirely superficial and both clubs draw support from all sections of the Western Australia society, not least of all Fremantle which is now occupied by middle class, gentrified society.[25]

The club's marketing, relying on the language and imagery of a white, male dockworker, resonated positively in its supporters' minds, despite Fremantle's main demographic being middle-class. Even in Fremantle's official chronology of events, the only person mentioned that resembles a dock worker is Tom Edwards, killed famously at the height of local union power on Fremantle's waterfront.[26] Edwards was struck dead by a policeman on 4 May 1919 while trying to shield a union leader from police violence.[27] The assault occurred when a flotilla from Perth tried to quash strike action by Fremantle lumpers (dockworkers) refusing to unload a ship until a quarantine period for Spanish flu had expired. Edwards is remembered in Fremantle as a martyr who died for his family, fellow workers and Fremantle community. After his mile-long funeral procession, the Tom Edwards memorial fountain was constructed in Fremantle. While not naming Edwards, Fremantle Football Club's marketing consultants looked to a particular romanticised past of waterfront workers' struggle in developing the clubs colours, logo and nautical identity.[28] Rather than develop an animal mascot typical of the Australian Football League, the marketing consultants invented the 'Dockers' nickname and inserted a docker (a strong man who loads and unloads ships) in the club logo. The club's earlier football jumper included an anchor and shipping lights in a dominant display that also represented the national flag of Fremantle's large Italian community. The club logo still sports the Dockers 'D' and anchor. It is also worth noting the chorus of the Fremantle Dockers' seafaring ditty with its perverse appeal – given the fate of Tom Edwards – to masculine violence through giving opponents the Freo Heave Ho (Freo being the popular abbreviation for Fremantle):

> Fre-o way to go, hit 'em real hard and send them below
> Fre-o give 'em the old heave ho,
> We are the Fre-o Dockers
> Fre-o way to go, hit 'em real hard and send them below

Fre-o give 'em the old heave ho, we are the Freo Dockers[29]

Evidence that this production of waterfront working-men's solidarity resonated with the local public was demonstrated when a crowd of more than 12,000 marched through Fremantle in August 1997 to oppose a proposal that the Docker's clubrooms be relocated from Fremantle Oval to Subiaco.[30] This demonstration indicated a deep horizontal comradeship in Fremantle's imagined community, a sense of loyalty to the hard-working men who ensured colonial prosperity by loading and unloading the ships moving between the western gateway to Australia and other parts of the world. Loyalty to the colony and devotion to an empire stretching back to antiquity is a metanarrative sign-posted all along Fremantle's High Street in the form of sacred-soliciting neoclassical artefacts, up to the War Memorial on Monument Hill. As the sun rises behind the memorial on Anzac Day, people assemble to be reminded of stories about the egalitarian sacrifices of their community's members starting with a dawn military landing on the beach at Gallipoli in 1915.[31] The beach frequently features in heroic Anzac stories, whether they involve the community's best young men charging across the beach to be killed again and again by strangers, or men and women rallying to the beach to fight – at any cost – a looming threat from well-resourced enemies from across the sea. Beaches are frontiers of social division in the Anzac legend. There is no hospitality for those outside the beach frontier.

Notes

1   G. A. Haimes, 'Organizational culture and identity: A case study from the Australian Football League', PhD thesis, Victoria University, Melbourne, 2006, p. 73.

2   B. Anderson, *Imagined Communities: Reflections on the Origin and Spread of Nationalism,* Verso, London, 1991, pp. 15–16.

3   Transcript of Fremantle Council meeting on 24 June 2009. See Appendix 004 in T. Kerr, 'Representing ecological threats and negotiating green built environment', PhD thesis, Curtin University, 2012.

4   *Fremantle Herald,* 19 September 2009, p. 11.

5   *2006 Census of population and housing,* ABS, Canberra, 2007, viewed 3 May 2010, <http://www.censusdata.abs.gov.au>.

6   Ibid.

7   T. Kerr & S. Cox, *Setting up the Nyoongar Tent Embassy: a Report on Perth Media,* Ctrl-Z Press, Perth, 2013.

8   P. Statham-Drew, *James Stirling: Admiral and Founding Governor of Western Australia,* University of Western Australia Press, Crawley, 2003, p. 144.

9   J. K. Ewers, *The Western Gateway: A History of Fremantle,* University of Western Australia Press, Nedlands, 1971, p. 6.

10   Ibid., p. 13.

11   Ibid., pp. 94–129.

12   There is a noticeable shift towards recognition of Aboriginal pre-history in the Fremantle area in municipality sponsored writing in the late 1990s compared to earlier works such as the early 1970s celebration of Fremantle's history in becoming The Western Gateway of Australia for European trade and communications; such as Ewers, *The Western Gateway.*

13   R. Porter, J. Moorhouse, A. Kins & B. Peddie, *Our Place: Cultural Policy and Plan,* City of Fremantle, Fremantle, 1999, p. 12.

14   Ibid., p. 21.

15   Ibid., p. 13.

16   J. Hartley, 'Expatriation: Useful astonishment as cultural studies', *Cultural Studies,* vol. 6, no. 3, 1992, p. 454.

17   J. Hartley, 'A State of Excitement: Western Australia and the America's Cup', *Cultural Studies,* vol. 2, no. 1, 1988, pp. 117–26.

18   Ibid., p. 125.

19   Ewers, *The Western Gateway,* pp. 111–65.

20   D. Cahill, 'New-class discourse and construction of left-wing elites', in M. Sawer & B. Hindness (eds), *Us and Them: Anti-elitism in Australia,* API Network, Australia Research Institute, Perth, 2004, pp. 86–94.

21   Porter et al., *Our Place,* p. 14.

22   M. M. Bakhtin, *The Dialogic Imagination: Four Essays,* C. Emerson & M. Holquist (trans), University of Texas Press, Austin, 1981, pp. 261–63.

23   Haimes, 'Organizational culture and identity', pp. 109–245.

24   Ibid., p. 141.

25 Ibid., p. 143.
26 Fremantle City Library, *Fremantle time line*, City of Fremantle, Fremantle, viewed 9 January 2014, <Retrieved from http://www.fremantle.wa.gov. au/files/c78e3d64-db14–4b33–8113–9dbd016f5789/Fremantle_time_line. doc>.
27 B. Bunbury, *Caught in Time: Talking Australian History*. Fremantle Arts Centre Press, Fremantle, 2006, pp. 74–80.
28 Haimes, 'Organizational culture and identity: A case study from the Australian Football League', pp. 153–75.
29 Ibid., p. 173.
30 Ibid., p. 150.
31 *Dawn Service*, Australian War Memorial, Canberra, viewed 10 January 2014, <https://www.awm.gov.au/commemoration/anzac/dawn/>.

OUR BEACHES

Photograph by Prapti Widinugraheni

'It's D-Day as developers continue their assault on our beaches, with the mother of all developments, the $10 billion North Port Quay'[1]

Fremantle Herald

After representing Fremantle for nineteen years in the Western Australian parliament, a relieved-looking Jim McGinty handed his resignation letter to House Speaker Grant Woodhams. This humble public exit took place below the limestone edifice of Parliament House in Perth on Friday, 3 April 2009.[2] The once-formidable power broker walked away from a jewel in the Australian

Labor Party's crown, the union-supported seat held consistently by members of the party since 1924.[3] Although former-attorney-general McGinty had been accused of many things, such as not reigning in former-planning-minister Alannah MacTiernan over coastal development,[4] he had stood firm with his premier against North Port Quay. For this, he and Carpenter were called a couple of 'lethargic, lefty naysayers'[5] with their 'put-your-head-in-the-sand'[6] rejection of the project. But with Carpenter out of the way, and McGinty on his way out of Fremantle, the North Port Quay consortium saw an opportunity to breach the social frontier that had so obviously formed against it over the previous ten months. They aimed to do this by providing an expensive public demonstration of shared perspective with the people about 'our environment' in Fremantle.[7] Fifteen days after McGinty's resignation was announced, North Port Quay's advertising campaign resumed with an image, not of the project, but of a perspective from Port Beach looking past a lone surfer across an empty sea to Fremantle Port's container stack and seawall. The image was shot from the same location where North Port Quay's most public opponents and then successful politicians – Colin Barnett, Lynn MacLaren and Adele Carles – had stood against the project. The consortium's new advertisement suggested this was 'the perfect place for North Port Quay'.[8] The project would be an 'investment in our environment, jobs and our way of life' in Fremantle,[9] rather than the coastal-lifestyle property development that the consortium had suggested in previous campaigns. The coastal tagline in this new advertisement, 'It just makes sense', and the lack of project renderings, worked to suggest that the consortium valued open beaches and respected an idealised Fremantle in which little would change with the arrival of North Port Quay. The advertisement's tranquil blond, with her surfboard borne like a child on hip, suggested the consortium's answer to a symbolic motherhood challenge put to it by *Fremantle Herald* in July 2008, when its front page carried an image of Adele Carles and Lynn MacLaren wanting 'to put a protective green blanket over Freo's beaches'.[10] Around this time, the newspaper had also published an opinion piece by Mary Jenkins saying that North Port Quay seemed like 'the end of Fremantle and our beaches as we know them'.[11] This was followed up with a political advertisement showing Carles and MacLaren standing on 'our beaches' taking 'Green Action'.[12] 'Protect our beaches' was demonstrated literally and figuratively, with the Greens' women standing on Port Beach to defy housing over the seabed as well as other issues such as lead exports through Fremantle Port.[13] These formidable women standing defiantly on and for 'our beaches' was an image sufficiently ambiguous[14] to represent a wide range of public demands and to constitute a symbolic frontier that divided Fremantle into two communities: those 'for' the beaches and those 'against'. The community of people for the beaches was represented by public expressions of this support. For local people, such as Bryn Davis writing into the local paper, 'our waterfronts' formed a part of memory that was integral to local popular identity: 'This includes our beaches, the Swan River and Fremantle Harbour'.[15] Like many others, Davis had made an emotional investment in 'our beaches', making this object much more than itself:[16] this movement against North Port Quay was not supported so much by the beach itself, but by people's memory of their days at the beach:

> When I was a child I could walk all the way from South
> Beach to Cicerellos, following the beach or seawall.
> With my friends I could explore or fish almost anywhere

along the harbour…We have been physically cut off from much of our access to the beach and we are now being visually cut off from the water, for example by… North Port Quay…which brings up quite a number of unanswered problems. For example, the effects of climate change and rising sea levels, the erosion of beaches north of the development, the massive traffic problems that would arise when a population of 15,000 to 20,000 new residents are installed, and associated parking problems from this massive increase of traffic, the huge disruption throughout the whole development stage (up to 10 years), the blocking of the views of the ocean, etc. Also what happened to the ruling that there should be a 100 metre setback from the coast for any development?[17]

Taking a stand for 'our beaches' incorporated a variety of complaints against North Port Quay as well as demands for solutions to broader social problems, as expressed in this letter to *Fremantle Herald* by Charles Dortch about why 'our beaches are infinitely more important' than coastal developments such as North Port Quay:

This ongoing confrontation on our coast is yet another case of a crucially important resource being exposed through human machination and commercial greed.

Professor Peter Newman consistently fails to grasp this, despite his repeated usage (in innumerable con-texts) of the buzz word 'sustainability', so favoured these days by politicians, bureaucrats, developers and their academic hirelings.[18]

Seeing his reputation under attack as this community formed against North Port Quay, Newman attempted in late August 2008 to breach the developing social frontier by positioning himself with the people of 'our beaches' while saying that the project would improve the beaches:

> Many people including Charles Dortch and Jim McGinty (in his newsletter) have written saying we must protect our beaches from NPQ. NPQ will not harm beaches. It has been redesigned after public consultation to now enable Sand Tracks to be part of the protected beach system (it is presently in the port area), Port and Leighton will be improved by expanding their sand base, and three new beaches will be created. How can I be so sure? Because the coastal engineering concepts in the Hillarys Marina and Mandurah Marina were done by the same people and these have worked to protect and create new beaches.[19]

Around this time, public debate shifted from a discussion of reasons to protect our beaches to a debate over who could actually be trusted to protect our beaches. This was when two full, facing-page advertisements about our beaches appeared in the *Fremantle Herald*. The first asked readers 'Who can you trust to protect our beaches?' and the second providing an answer from Greens candidates Andrew Sullivan and Adele Carles: 'WE WILL FIGHT THEM ON THE BEACHES!'[20] While reiterating that there were people on the other side of this coastal community to fight, Carles and Sullivan wanted social action in the form of electoral votes for 'our beaches, our community, our democracy, our future'.[21] Indeed, a World War 2 metaphor supported this

populist call 'to fight them on the beaches' in the news summary
for May printed in the final edition of *Fremantle Herald* for 2008:

> It's D-Day as developers continue their assault on our
> beaches, with the mother of all developments, the $10
> billion North Port Quay, announced for Rous Head.
> NPQ's six manmade islands will house 20,000 people
> and have shops, schools, hotels and boat marinas on 345
> hectares of seabed, all surrounded by a 3.5 kilometre
> seawall to hold back rising sea levels.[22]

After the community had been called to defend its beaches
against external threats, the NPQ consortium retreated for several
months to rethink its public-relations strategy. If it couldn't beat
the people of our beaches, it would attempt to join them in the
Fremantle by-election brought about by McGinty's resignation.
The consortium launched its new campaign, featuring Port Beach
and the tagline 'It just makes sense', on large billboards around
Fremantle. It also bought space to publish the advertisement over
two facing pages in the *Fremantle Herald* on 18 and 25 April 2009,
and in the *Fremantle Gazette* on 21 April and 28 April. Despite
the investment, this grand strategy appeared to fail to overcome
the damage done to North Port Quay's image in previous public
encounters. David Hawks said the advertisement on a billboard
near Pioneer Park was 'presuming to define Fremantle's future'.[23]
A modified version of the two-page advertisement was published
in *The West Australian* on 6 May. The Port Beach background
was maintained but the distant lone surfer in the advertisement
for Fremantle audiences was replaced with an Australian celeb-
rity in the foreground. Former-test-cricketer Geoff Marsh was
photographed successfully defending his wicket in an apparently

enjoyable game of beach cricket with healthy, young people on the beach, with sea and the Fremantle port facilities in the background. Geoff Marsh was portrayed as an ideal local father wanting to protect beaches for future generations. In words attributed to him:

> Western Australians love going to the beach. It's a great place to have fun with the family and that's why I think our beaches need protecting for future generations to enjoy.[24]

Marsh seems to know an awful lot about North Port Quay. He says it will create 4,500 jobs, extend Port Beach, create two more family beaches, protect Port Beach from erosion and use renewable energy to power homes and businesses. The same advertisement tagline about NPQ being an 'investment in our environment, jobs and way of life' then appears above Geoff Marsh's signature, just above the NPQ logo and tagline: 'It just makes sense'. North Port Quay is thus an ideal coastal development for right-thinking Western Australians.

For apparently left-leaning locals within the Fremantle electorate, however, Adele Carles was positioned in the Greens by-election advertisements as the true protector of 'our' beaches: 'She is known for her passionate campaigns to save our beaches'.[25] This idea of a true protector was supported by Socialist Alliance Sam Wainwright's campaign, which advertised who the people of 'our beaches' were, by suggesting who they weren't: 'No North Port Quay – don't privatise our beaches'; and 'Reject developers' greed gone mad!'[26] The further the by-election campaign progressed, the more it became clear that it was untenable to position North Port Quay with the people of 'our beaches'. This failure, despite substantial financial investment in persuading the community otherwise, was due to the resilience of the social frontier. This resilience was constituted out of locals' prior knowledge of coastal-development scandals and property-ownership rights, as well as their knowledge of beaches from both discursive and sensual encounters. Sedimentary layers of knowledge had developed over time to make beaches integral, symbolic borders of Australian identity.

This knowledge coincided with fond memories of beach experiences in the subjectivities of many voters, who would choose Carles to represent Fremantle in the Western Australian Parliament. This subjectivity relied on Carles being known as a true defender of 'our beaches' in the face of their annexation and destruction by developments such as North Port Quay. The threat of North Port Quay sweeping across the beach in a new wave of colonisation created a variety of demands in the electorate to protect aspects of Fremantle from the project, and these demands constituted a unity that became most apparent during the by-election. Adele Carles took to the stage as the people's honest defender against the threat of coastal property development: 'Political donations from property developers, the big parties accept them. We don't.'[27] Her stance was met with cries of support and thunderous applause. 'If elected I'll be pressing for strict restrictions [on political donations],' she said. The North Port Quay developer 'has no more right to the seabed than you or I. This is public seabed.' Carles suggested the project was a sick joke, 'no different from us asking the government for a free block of land in Kings Park. We would be laughed out of town if we tried it.' She also reiterated common readings of the project as 'a Dubai-style development', and a 'theme park for the wealthy' that would 'be the kiss of death for our working port of Fremantle'.[28] Various demands against North Port Quay were articulated in the by-election debate in relation to the future of Fremantle's port, environmental threats and the difference between Carles and Labor's candidate. Audience applause suggested that speaking against North Port Quay was the popular thing to do, as the by-election debate and electoral campaigns encouraged local participation in policy making and the people's participation in democratic governance. Although images of Greg Poland's monumental vision had been kept out of advertisements for North Port Quay during the by-election campaign, the project was still inscribed with threatening meanings that evoked powerful responses in the Fremantle electorate. In desperation, Poland wrote to the *Fremantle Herald* to limit the damage being inflicted on his project from its involvement in the by-election campaign. His letter, published a week before polling day, attempted to destabilise the discursive frontier that had formed against North Port Quay threatening Port Beach. The letter suggested Poland already knew Carles would win the by-election despite the considerable resources his people had pitched against her campaign. 'I have to correct the record,' he wrote, '[regarding] Greens candidate Adele Carles' statement that North Port Quay would destroy Port Beach'.[29] This was not what the consortium's research suggested, he said: 'The truth is that Port Beach will be extended by nearly a kilometre and its sand movement stabilised if North Port Quay goes ahead'. But this game of truth had been lost, and Poland's letter went on to make a last-ditch public suggestion of unity with the soon-to-be-victorious Greens around the object of ecological modernisation: 'The Greens want to reduce WA's greenhouse gas emissions and promote sustainable communities, where low-emission forms of transport, such as public transport, cycling and walking are the norm,' he wrote. 'I want all of these things as well and with the support of world-renowned sustainability expert Peter Newman, I have committed my time and effort to achieving this.' The mover and shaker behind North Port Quay said he hoped 'to work closely with the Greens and all Western Australians who share the common goal of sustainable development based on renewable energy'.[30]

After the by-election, Greg Poland complained there had been misinformation about the project's location in the media and among politicians in the by-election coverage.[31] 'Despite what has been said,' he contended, 'it will not be built on Port Beach but at the end of Rous Head.'[32]

Notes

1   *Fremantle Herald*, 27 December 2008, p. 16.
2   *Jim McGinty resignation Perth*, Associated Press, New York, viewed 14 January 2014, <http://bigstory.ap.org/photo/jim-mcginty-resignation-perth>.
3   *Electorate profiles: District of Fremantle (South Metropolitan Region)*, Parliament of Western Australia, Perth, viewed 13 January 2014, <http://www.parliament.wa.gov.au/intranet/LibPages.nsf/589198976847966848256e5a0008666d/bd2598dc79877cb2c82574a90025f0b9?OpenDocument#Successive%20Members%20of%20Parliament>.
4   *Fremantle Herald*, 23 May 2009, p. 7.
5   *The West Australian*, 31 May 2008, p. 22.
6   Ibid., p. 2.
7   *Fremantle Herald*, 18 April 2009, pp. 6–7.
8   Ibid.
9   Ibid.
10 *Fremantle Herald*, 5 July 2008, p. 1.
11 *Fremantle Herald*, 26 July 2008, p. 5.
12 *Fremantle Herald*, 16 August 2008, p. 3.
13 Ibid.
14 The theoretical term for this mechanism supporting the formation of popular social movements is 'empty signifier'. Laclau, *On Populist Reason*, pp. 104–20.
15 *Fremantle Herald*, 23 August 2008, p. 11.
16 J. Copjec, *Imagine There's No Woman: Ethics and Sublimation*, MIT Press, Cambridge, Massachusetts, 2004, pp. 41–2.
17 *Fremantle Herald*, 23 August 2008, p. 11.

18   Ibid., p. 16.
19   *Fremantle Herald*, 30 August 2008, p. 6.
20   Ibid., pp. 16–17.
21   Ibid.
22   *Fremantle Herald*, 27 December 2008, pp. 16–17.
23   *Fremantle Herald*, 25 April 2009, p. 35.
24   *The West Australian*, 6 May 2009, pp. 16–17.
25   *Fremantle Gazette*, 5 May 2009, p. 7.
26   *Fremantle Herald*, 9 May 2009, p. 8.
27   Transcript of Fremantle by-election debate on 5 May 2009. See Appendix
     007 in T. Kerr, 'Representing ecological threats and negotiating green built
     environment', PhD thesis, Curtin University, 2012.
28   Ibid.
29   *Fremantle Herald*, 9 May 2009, p. 4.
30   Ibid.
31   *Fremantle Gazette*, 26 May 2009, p. 5.
32   Ibid.

FREMANTLE MOTHER

Greens campaign advertisement, as it appeared in *Fremantle Gazette*

'Much of what you've heard has been the sort of misleading talk you would expect in an election campaign. As Communications Manager for North Port Quay I would like to point out the facts.'[1]

Anne Burns

Adele Carles was being groomed to win Fremantle for the Greens well before McGinty announced his resignation. The *Fremantle Herald*'s New Year edition reminded readers to look out for her:

> Green Machine is how environmental pin-up boy Bob Brown sees local candidate Adele Carles after she almost snags Fremantle from Labor veteran Jim McGinty in the state election. He promises the national body's full support next time after she records the highest-ever Green vote for a lower house seat in Australia. At one point during election night the ABC announces she's snatched the traditionally safe Labor seat before realising its error.[2]

A few more votes would have put Carles in front of the Liberal party's candidate, leading to a landslide win for the Greens over Labor in the seat in 2008 on preference distribution. Facing this scenario in the 2009 by-election, the Liberal party determined not to run a candidate. Just months into their term in government, it seemed sensible for the Liberals to avoid tempering news of a Labor heartland defeat with the loss of their own candidate to the Greens. Therefore all eyes were on Labor to see whether its internal elite would persuade Fremantle Mayor Peter Tagliaferri to nominate for pre-selection.[3] Tagliaferri was persuaded to run for Labor and the party's central Administration Committee unanimously chose him ahead of local long-standing members.[4] State media then shifted its attention to a close electoral contest between Tagliaferri and Carles.

Eleven candidates had been nominated for the Fremantle by-election by noon on Friday 17 April.[5] As Labor's new man, Peter

Tagliaferri turned up for the official draw of ballot paper positions in a light-blue shirt, sleeves rolled-up, and blue-striped tie. Not all candidates were there, but Adele Carles showed up in her usual smart, black skirt suit with husband and child in tow. Tagliaferri and Carles crossed the floor of the cramped reception in the local Australian Electoral Commission office to shake hands and kiss each other. So began the electoral contest for Fremantle.

In the meantime the North Port Quay consortium was not just busily appropriating the beach perspective that had worked so well for MacLaren and Carles in the previous election, it was also devising publicity to associate the project with its own formidable middle-aged woman. Former political editor of *The West Australian* Anne Burns[6] came to the foreground at this time as the project spokesperson to take on Adele Carles.[7] The professional lobbyist and partner of Halden Burns told the press that the consortium would continue its campaign to win official support throughout the by-election. She also downplayed suggestions that the consortium was funding candidates.[8] In the paradoxical fashion of a lobbyist, Burns reportedly said the beach advertisements and billboards for North Port Quay were being put up in the campaign because the project was too big to become a political football.[9] The front page of *Fremantle Herald* on 2 May read:

> North Port Quay is shaping up as a Fremantle by-election issue with its consortium buying advertising to promote the project ahead of the May 16 poll.
>
> At least three independent candidates publicly back the futuristic project and Labor's Peter Tagliaferri is "keeping an open mind".
>
> But the Greens' Adele Carles is opposed outright to the plan to fill in ocean off Rous Head in North

Fremantle and build four artificial islands topped with apartment towers...[10]

Anne Burns called on Adele Carles to retract a 'statement that NPQ would destroy Port Beach'.[11] Carles responded by saying that North Port Quay had not undertaken a proper environmental assessment and other marina developments had ended in disaster. 'I can't believe we are even having this discussion,' Carles said in response to Burns' demand. 'We haven't learnt anything.'[12] Meanwhile, North Port Quay's representatives were lobbying hard behind the scenes and Labor's new opposition leader, Eric Ripper, was reportedly looking forward to receiving a formal submission on the project.[13] This kind of news was not helping Peter Tagliaferri's campaign. Carles accused Labor of back-flipping on the project. She said Labor was opening the door to this 'Dubai-style' development which would 'be an environmental disaster'. Tagliaferri refused to condemn North Port Quay. Instead, he tried to shift it off the campaign agenda by locating the project outside Fremantle's electoral boundary and way into the future, where it may be blocked by bureaucratic hurdles.[14] Yet his attempts to locate the project outside the campaign were repeatedly frustrated by the consortium's determination to put North Port Quay back in.

Full-page advertisements for independent candidates Nik Varga and Steve Boni first appeared in the *Fremantle Gazette*'s 21 April edition, the first edition to publish North Port Quay's two-page beach advertisement. An uncanny similarity could be ascribed to the advertisements for Boni and Varga – one which couldn't be put down to their templates which were so obviously different. Perhaps it was their opening statements beginning with 'I' and their persistent use of the first person. Or perhaps it was the candidates' appearance in chambray shirts alongside impoverished images of Fremantle – photographs without voters; candidates without friends. Regardless, full-page advertisements for Varga and Boni appeared in Fremantle newspapers in a series of spectacular coincidences: both advertisements appeared in a 21 April edition, then both appeared in editions on 2, 5, 9, 12 and 16 May. With intimate knowledge of press advertising, it was little wonder the *Fremantle Herald* told readers: 'Messrs Boni and Varga say they have not received any funding from NPQ.'[15]

Nik Varga's advertisement looked like it had come from a Liberal party archive, showing true-blue colonial heritage topped off with Australian flags.[16] Expressing colonial mercantile tradition through an image of the Fremantle market's facade, this former Liberal voter was taking electoral matters into his own hands because 'the port city' had stagnated since America's Cup. The city no longer met Varga's lifestyle expectations, which is why he headed 'to Hillarys Boat Harbour on the weekends' (the founding project of Strzelecki Holdings,[17] the driving force behind North Port Quay). Varga wanted North Port Quay to go ahead to create thousands of jobs. At the same time, he was against the earlier Three Harbours proposal because it would remove public beaches, put more traffic on the roads and 'ruin the views'.[18] He also appealed for the conservative vote by wanting more police on the streets and for Fremantle to keep its port, but without the unpopular live-sheep and lead exports. In waging an expensive campaign with little chance of victory, Varga was out to capture Liberal voters and shift their preferences towards Tagliaferri. Varga said he would not preference the Greens because they 'oppose growth, they oppose change and they oppose making Fremantle a more vibrant place'.[19] For added vibrancy, North Port Quay's billboard headline was mixed into Varga's advertising headline: 'For Fremantle's future don't vote greens.'[20]

Steve Boni's advertisements were concerned about 'vibrancy': 'The vibrancy of this historic port city is being lost.'[21] They also seemed to celebrate a lifestyle based on empty cafes, ocean sunsets and powerboats. Boni was fond of Fremantle's fishing-boat harbour, cappuccino strip and footy team. He stood for preserving Fremantle's character while developing its vibrancy. He used the metaphor of his migration journey from Italy to Fremantle to charm migrant voters and support the idea of 'Giving North Port Quay a fair go': 'As an Italian-Australian I understand the importance of giving someone a fair go.'[22] Like Varga, Boni also stood for the popular demands of making Fremantle safer and retaining its port, but without lead exports.

Standing against lead exports was a key platform in Peter Tagliaferri's 'Putting Fremantle First' campaign, which suggested he was trusted by the city's families. Pictured on a mundane couch, her arms enfolding her young son and daughter, 'Sara Jooste, Mum', appeared to say: 'Peter was one of the first to stand up against lead in Freo port...I know we can trust Fremantle's future to him.'[23] Yet, this advertisement for Mayor Tagliaferri was undermined on the same page by Deputy Mayor John Dowson's cross advertisement, headed 'Peter Tagliaferri Putting Fremantle Last'.[24] Local endorsements for Tagliaferri in campaign advertising were matched by an advertised demand that he 'resign immediately' from the mayoral position for reasons including a hypocritical position on North Port Quay: 'You call yourself an "environmental campaigner" when you refused to reject the proposed total destruction of Port Beach by NPQ.'[25] This advertisement included the names of 111 people who 'paid for this ad'.[26] High up the list was Kim Dravnieks, a key supporter of Carles' campaign. A few days earlier she had stood with Carles on Port Beach for a photo of Green women against North Port Quay.[27]

Adele Carles was photographed with family for advertisements showing that she 'cares about the people of Fremantle'.[28] This image of care began with Carles holding hands with her daughters in the foreground, husband Francois slightly behind: 'As a mother I understand that family security is a big issue for us all'.[29] The Carles family appeared walking towards the camera on a Fremantle street[30] then as a portrait in a Fremantle park.[31] Campaign images of the family authenticated Carles as a successful Fremantle mother, calling on voters to support political change 'so she can continue her hard work in critical areas such as protecting Fremantle Markets tenancies, keeping our port working, and opposing off-shore housing developments'.[32] Carles was an ideal Fremantle mother, who did not fall for the suggestion that her mother image was inconsistent with Greens policy. In the by-election debate held at the University of Notre Dame, an audience member put an emotionally charged question to Carles: 'Do you suggest that prostitution is a good employment opportunity and would you be happy if your children went into that?'[33] Carles maintained her usual calm confidence: 'Of course the Greens don't advocate prostitution as a great career option.'[34] The Greens policy on regulating prostitution was about public health and work safety, 'and those workers have rights just like other Australian workers do'.[35] Community allegiance was sought by Carles through her understanding of life's daily struggles, 'as a working mother'.[36]

In Our Lady's Drill Hall that evening, Carles stood out among the ten participating candidates in putting North Port Quay on the debate agenda. She did this right after establishing her party's moral position on political donations, stating that they did not accept money from property developers.

With confidence in the Greens' environmental record and the crowd at her feet, Carles turned the tables on Tagliaferri's campaign platform:

> Lead exports. Let's not forget that it was the Labor government that got us into this mess a year ago when they approved the plan. When the Greens challenged them in parliament, we were ridiculed…Now they have back flipped for political gain. The Greens are the only party that has stood against lead in Fremantle from the very start.[37]

Through the image of a protective mother caring for Fremantle, Carles appropriated the law-and-order platform typically associated with Liberal campaigns and linked it to Greens healthcare policy:

> I support increased funding for police services in Fremantle to keep our community safe. As a mother I know that family security is a big issue for all of us. I also support the retention of a 24-hour emergency department at Fremantle Hospital as an important regional centre, of course we need a well-funded Fremantle Hospital.[38]

Carles' opener closed with a call for change after '85 years of Labor', and a promise: 'if you vote Green you'll get an independent voice in our parliament'.[39] An hour into the debate, candidates were asked whether they supported North Port Quay and whether they received campaign resources to do so. Carles answered with a giggle that she had not received any donations from the developers. This was met with laughter and an extensive applause from audience members.

Sam Wainwright's heroic egalitarian response to these questions produced so much audience reaction that he could hardly speak over the thunderous applause and cheers egging him on:

1:17:58 Sam Wainwright: As Jan said we live in Australia not Hong Kong. We do not need to fill in the ocean floor to create space for housing for rich people and in so doing privatise something that belongs to all of us. Not just to the people of Fremantle, but don't the people of Midland and Armadale have a right to attend a beach and not be overlooked by yuppies peering over their, peering over their balconies…

1:18:17 Laughter and applause

1:18:17 Sam Wainwright: as well. I mean don't they. I mean…

1:18:20 Laughter, applause and cheers

1:18:26 Sam Wainwright: the mind boggles…and this guff about it being carbon neutral. What about the millions of litres of diesel that are going to have to be burnt to dump rocks onto the ocean floor. If Peter Newman wants a sustainable village build it at Armadale or Midland for people who really need it. And if

1:18:41 Applause and cheers

1:18:41 Sam Wainwright: If

1:18:42 Applause and cheers

1:18:44 Sam Wainwright: If I tell you what. If

1:18:46 Applause and cheers

1:18:48 Sam Wainwright: If

1:18:48 Applause and cheers

1:18:49 Sam Wainwright: If if the jokers proposing this thing are fair dinkum…they are going to have to drive their bulldozers over bodies. I'll give you the tip. All right![40]

Wainwright had the audience 'eating out of his hand', read the front page of *Fremantle Herald*:[41] 'But audience cheers won't mean much come polling day – it's a two-horse race and pundits gave the debating points to the Greens' Adele Carles over Labor candidate Peter Tagliaferri.'[42] North Port Quay was all over the front page and referred to throughout this 9 May edition:

> Asked whether they'd received donations from NPQ's backers all 10 (Rosemary Lorrimar did not turn up) replied "no".
>
> Nik Varga and Steve Boni said they were definitely in favour of the project while Mr Tagliaferri, Carmelo Zagami, Rob Totten and Julie Hollett were "keeping an open mind".
>
> Jan ter Horst, Ms Carles and Mr Wainwright opposed it.[43]

Front-page coverage of the by-election debate was framed by suggestions of wrongdoing by North Port Quay supporters. The top headline, 'NPQ lobbyist advised campaign', related to how 'former Labor MP John Halden – a paid lobbyist for the North Port Quay project – has emerged as a behind-the-scenes adviser to Fremantle by-election candidate Nik Varga'.[44] In the right of this frame another headline, 'ACCC wags finger at carbon claims', referred to the Australian Competition and Consumer Commission telling the North Port Quay consortium to 'tone down its carbon-neutral claims' or face a hefty fine. Just a week from the by-election, Fremantle's most popular newspaper suggested North Port Quay's proponents had been caught out attempting to corrupt democratic process and the meaning of carbon neutrality.

Bob Brown flew into town to associate his symbolic force, of environmental activism against corporate greed, with this 'very special election'.[45] With Carles, he outlined a sustainability vision differentiated from North Port Quay's by building sustainable suburbs on land, by bike riding over car driving and by installation of solar panels and insulation in every Australian home starting 'with the poorer houses and moving up'.[46] The Greens' sustainability vision was more likely to appeal to current voters than North Port Quay's sustainability vision that seemed to be written for a constituency yet to arrive in Fremantle. Architect and future local councillor Andrew Sullivan also got behind Carles, saying it 'beggars belief that so many politicians have been suckered in by flashy marketing and hired guns being paraded about town by the NPQ developers':[47]

> Calls for a "fair-go" by the developer's PR machine remind me of cigarette salesmen…snake-oil peddling by-election candidates jumping on the medicine-man's wagon…It's time to bury the NPQ folly at sea and move back to the land to fulfil our needs.[48]

The consortium tried to counter the wave of public support building behind Carles with a new two-page advertisement showing concerned radio personality Jane Marwick looking at classified advertisements for jobs to be created by its project. But the battle for North Port Quay had already been lost.[49] A week before polling day, ABC1 broadcast news of Carles' concerns over Fremantle by-election candidates receiving financial support from North Port Quay.[50] Links were then drawn between NPQ and Nik Varga's real estate business, suggesting that he was hiding from the media, as it became apparent that this was yet another instance of big property developer versus coastal community. The piece also suggested that claims around carbon neutrality were false and complicit in NPQ's legitimisation strategy. Four days out from the poll, the front page of *Fremantle Gazette* suggested that secret political donations from property developers had become the key by-election issue.[51] *The West Australian* joined in with an article, 'People in North Port Quay ads feel duped', about 'people photographed as part of an advertisement for the $10 billion North Port Quay development' claiming they were misrepresented.[52] The article focused on the personal impact of unethical behaviour by NPQ's proponents, which 'Communication Manager for NPQ, Anne Burns, defended' by way of a 'surprising… misunderstanding'.[53]

Anne Burns made a last stand for North Port Quay in advertisements in *The West Australian* on the eve[54] and the day of the election.[55] These half-page advertisements suggested a letter from Anne Burns to the people of Fremantle, who 'may have heard a lot about North Port Quay in the last few weeks of the Fremantle by-election'.[56] With a large head-shot of Burns superimposed against the sea, near a sailing boat apparently passing Port Beach and a stack of shipping containers, the advertisement asked voters to trust this capable woman's endorsement of North Port Quay because it 'just makes sense'.[57] The letter from Burns argued that there were many important positive 'facts' about NPQ that needed to be pointed out amid the 'sort of misleading talk you would expect in an election campaign'. The letter closed with a reiteration of NPQ being envisaged as a 'world leader in sustainable development' and an appeal to voters: 'North Port Quay is asking for a fair go. When you vote, please keep these things in mind. Anne Burns'.[58] Meanwhile, Adele Carles was telling voters: 'The future of Fremantle is in our hands. This is the day that YOU can make the difference.'[59]

People turned out in droves to have their say at polling stations across Fremantle on 16 May.[60] How they voted depended on what they knew to be true.

Notes

1   *The West Australian*, 16 May 2009, p. 19.
2   *Fremantle Herald*, 3 January 2009, p. 8
3   W. Bowe, *Fremantle by-election: May 16*, Crikey, Melbourne, 2009, viewed 17 January 2014, <http://blogs.crikey.com.au/pollbludger/2009/04/03/fremantle-by-election-may-16/?wpmp_switcher=mobile&wpmp_tp=6>.
4   Ibid.
5   *District of Fremantle By-election: 16 May 2009*, Western Australian Electoral Commission, Perth, viewed 17 January 2014, <https://www.elections.wa.gov.au/sites/default/files/content/documents/2009_Fremantle_By-election_Report.pdf>.
6   Halden Burns, Perth, viewed 24 March 2015, <http://www.haldenburns.com.au >.
7   *Fremantle Gazette*, 5 May 2009, p. 3.
8   *Fremantle Herald*, 25 April 2009, p. 24.
9   *Fremantle Herald*, 2 May 2009, p. 1.
10 Ibid.
11 Ibid.
12 Ibid.
13 *Fremantle Herald*, 2 May 2009, p. 13.
14 Ibid.
15 Ibid.

16   Ibid., p. 12.

17   *About Us*, Strzelecki Group, Perth, 2009, viewed 22 January 2014, <http://www.strzeleckigroup.com.au/>.

18   *Fremantle Herald*, 2 May 2009, p. 12.

19   Ibid.

20   *Fremantle Gazette*, 12 May 2009, p. 10.

21   *Fremantle Gazette*, 21 April 2009, p. 26.

22   Ibid.

23   *Fremantle Herald*, 9 May 2009, p. 3.

24   Ibid.

25   *Fremantle Herald*, 9 May 2009, p. 6.

26   Ibid.

27   *Fremantle Gazette*, 5 May 2009, p. 3.

28   *Fremantle Gazette*, 12 May 2009, p. 9.

29   Ibid.

30   *Fremantle Gazette*, 5 May 2009, p. 7.

31   *Fremantle Gazette*, 12 May 2009, p. 9.

32   *Fremantle Gazette*, 5 May 2009, p. 7.

33   Fremantle by-election debate, 5 May 2009.

34   Ibid.

35   Ibid.

36   Ibid.

37   Ibid.

38   Ibid.

39   Ibid.

40   Ibid.

41   *Fremantle Herald*, 9 May 2009, p. 1.

42   Ibid.

43   *Fremantle Herald*, 9 May 2009, p. 3.

44   Ibid., p. 1.

45   *Fremantle Gazette*, 12 May 2009, p. 3.

46   *Fremantle Herald*, 9 May 2009, p. 2.

47   Ibid., p. 11.

48   Ibid.

49   *Fremantle Herald*, 9 May 2009, pp. 10–11.

50   ABC1 News WA on 9 May 2009.

51   *Fremantle Gazette*, 12 May 2009, p. 1.

52   *The West Australian*, 12 May 2009, p. 16.

53   Ibid.

54   *The West Australian*, 15 May 2009, p. 18.

55 *The West Australian*, 16 May 2009, p. 19.
56 Ibid.
57 Ibid.
58 Ibid.
59 Ibid., p. 5.
60 *District of Fremantle By-election: 16 May 2009*, Western Australian Electoral Commission, Perth, viewed 17 January 2014, <https://www.elections.wa.gov.au/sites/default/files/content/documents/2009_Fremantle_By-election_Report.pdf>.

TEMPLE TOWN

Photograph by author

'One always says to someone else that the sacred is secret. Its secrecy is always a matter of demonstration or performance.... After all, secrets cannot be secrets unless they are spoken about as such'.[1]

K. Gelder and J. Jacobs

'The Empire required rituals, which old boys enthusiastically espoused...These rituals kept millions of people in their place. To orchestrate them, the British Imperialists became impresarios, directing a great worldwide extravaganza'.[2]

P. J. Rich

Fantastic energy and public fortunes are invested in the renewal of community identity. On the day after Survival Day 2014, before fireworks exploded over Bathers Bay, Mayor Brad Pettitt presented a community group award to Fremantle Forever for helping stave off a municipal amalgamation imposed on it by the Barnett government.[3] Meanwhile, amid great pomp in Canberra, Peter Newman became an Officer of the Order of Australia for distinguished service to education – 'through contributions to urban design and transport sustainability' – and community.[4] Such awards and their ceremonies help constitute their communities as something seemingly real and sacrosanct; real subjectivity to social constructions.

People are subjected by an assemblage of heritage objects[5] as they idle through Fremantle's professionally presented ruins, supporting tourism and devotion.[6] As if its downtown colonial buildings were sacred, devotees have taken to the streets to defend them against redevelopment.[7] Uncanny encounters with incongruous objects, suggesting something secret, have been shown to solicit sacredness in seemingly secular Australia.[8]

In this vein, new arrivals walked across Bather's Beach, then through the dim passage of Whalers Tunnel in the early years of the Fremantle settlement. Many emerged from this tunnel, blinking in the sunlight, gazing directly down High Street to the front doors of the Church of St John the Evangelist in King's Square. In literature, Fremantle's threshold between land and water functions as a symbolic 'boundary between sleep and waking, the conscious and the unconscious'.[9] Professor Jon Stratton has described the threshold as restarting the lives of those passing through it, making them socially white while leaving others outside in limbo or to drown at sea.[10] Constructed in 1837 at great effort for a barely performing company, Whalers Tunnel was built at the architect Henry Reveley's insistence directly underneath the Round House despite the stone building's additional weight.[11] The Round House gaol stood over the new arrivals suggesting retribution while St John's Church offered redemption. The Round House is presented today by the City of Fremantle as the oldest remaining building in Western Australia. This twelve-sided structure, commanding the western perspective down High Street, has been described as the first symbol of British colonial occupancy for anyone approaching the settlement from sea, even though its functional focus was domesticity.[12] The Round House was a colonial manager's attempt to control the local human population through secular rather than religious authority. Yet it had insufficient scale for the Western Australia colonial project. Rather than operate as a permanent prison, the Round House functioned as one of the temporary holding facilities through which the invasive white community banished thousands of Aboriginal men into the horror, disease and death of the Rottnest Island offshore detention facility.[13] Putrefaction became purification at a distance in colonial symbolic order. Looking back through this order, the Round House and Whalers Tunnel form an entrance porch to the temple of white Australia.

Heading inland up High Street the first two blocks are largely deserted, enabling full view of a series of facades preserved to their neoclassical architectural peak. The original facades served the interests of their European owners in what was then a busy trading district. This 'aesthetics of elegance', disguising the presence of commercial enterprise, was replicated throughout the colonised world.[14] Fremantle's facades continue to make their building functions secret, such as the open-air car parks hidden by reproduced heritage frontage on Essex Street. On High Street they symbolise a prosperous heritage stretching back under the

Round House and across the ocean to the cradle of civilised knowledge in classical Europe. They enable the twenty-five-year-old University of Notre Dame, operating behind these heritage facades, to seem much older and European than it really is. With their mix of functionally redundant neoclassical columns and other icons, these facades reproduce commitment to an imagined classical origin and imagined truth of European colonial thought.[15] An example is the mock column mounted within a Masonic-temple triangle in the peak of the facade of the Return Services League Club Wyola at 81 High Street. Apparently, such emblems aided Freemasons'[16] search for 'the memory of beginnings' and King Solomon's Temple.[17] The Fremantle Town Hall, the New Edition Bookshop facade and other temple iconography in High Street form a lingering Masonic style that was 'the essence of Neoclassicism'.[18]

A prominent slab mosaic in the centre of High Street, just before Kings Square, is comprised of mythical images telling stories of Fremantle. The mosaic's central slab contains the Round House and Whalers Tunnel as the focal point of this mythological arrangement. Above the Round House there is a large flying angel with an open book, suggesting the local Anglican mission to seafarers.[19] This angel with the open book, at the threshold of sea and land, also suggests a character in prophetic narrative about the annihilation of urban fornication throughout the world and the rise of a New Jerusalem. This particular angel orders John, the narrator, to eat the book then 'Rise and measure the temple of God, and the Altar, and them that worship within'.[20] Despite the moralising mosaic, Freo locals love telling tales of prostitution, incredible drug deals and drunken brawls along the High Street. But these stories are told in half whispers, with shy backward glances, because the events they describe have been tucked neatly away from public view. The undated, untitled and apparently un-authored mosaic helps to keep this side of Fremantle secret. Not disclosing the mosaic's recent production is part of the secret.

At the eastern end of the High Street Mall, Kings Square contains the Fremantle Town Hall and a new version of St John's Church surrounded by works of public art by and about European Australians. Over time, this square has been worked and reworked with a mix of artefacts, supporting the narration of Anglican, Masonic, local and national experience. On the east side of the square a large circular mosaic about locals inducted into the Sport Australia Hall of Fame represents local contribution fanning out into the Australia nation-building project. Kings Square was first established in the colony as a public reserve at what was then the far eastern end of High Street. However, within the first decade of settlement the square was appropriated by the Trustees of Church Property of St John's Church and a church built upon it by 1843.[21] This was torn down, and the existing church was constructed on the northern triangle of the square in 1879. Fremantle Council purchased the southern triangular portion of Kings Square from the church to build the Town Hall, which was completed in 1887. These alterations enabled an unimpeded view and traffic flow along High Street from the Round House up to Monument Hill, and later the construction of a tramline along this route. The Town Hall's construction, sponsored by Fremantle's mostly Masonic mercantile elite, opened up Fremantle's imperial passage.[22] As the influence of this elite declined amid the industrialisation of Fremantle at the turn of the century, the imperial passage of High Street was embellished. Fremantle's inner harbour replaced Bather's Bay as the point of international arrival and departure.[23] By the 1960s, a one-way road system had been constructed around Kings Square and a car park built within the square, interrupting the High Street line. However, with the rise of the heritage movement and supportive federal funding, the car park has since been removed and High Street's passage through Kings Square has been cleared. The direct passage along High Street from Bather's Bay to Monument Hill was restored by 2001 with the reopening of Whalers Tunnel to the public. Indeed, this passage towards the rising sun is expected to be clarified further if the Town Hall facade is extended with a civic-centre complex – a place for community assembly, designed by Kerry Hill Architects.[24]

Heading out of Kings Square through Queens Square and up the High Street hill, the Fremantle Prison appears on the right before a mix of institutional buildings and houses; then the street opens up at its peak to the manicured lawns of Monument Hill Memorial Reserve. The Fremantle War Memorial stands erect among the roses on this reserve as a symbolically fertile node of community regeneration and a reminder of the normality of undertaking overseas warfare for empire and nation. The memorial, a compromise between neoclassical column and divinely protective obelisk, commemorates World War 1, World War 2, the Korean War, Malayan emergency and the Vietnam War. Its construction was completed in 1928, replacing a large obelisk built for navigation purposes at the peak overlooking Fremantle in 1867. A conservation plan for the Monument Hill War Memorial was drafted in 2009, articulating concern about gambling, drinking, vandalism, football, fun and fireworks disrespecting its 'sacredness'.[25] After looking to religion for an understanding of environments that solicited the sacred, the plan's architects decided minimal change was needed to ensure the memorial continued to stimulate appropriate senses in its audience.[26] Memorialisation of international, rather than domestic, conflict would remain seemingly sacred.

Structures normalising institutional violence occupy the high spatial and moral ground in Fremantle: the Round House naturalises violence against those rendered domestically criminal while the War Memorial naturalises violence against those rendered aggressive or oppressive overseas. These and other structures that work to normalise acts of colonial and imperial violence are well preserved in Fremantle. It is much harder to find structures or public artefacts in Fremantle that work to naturalise Nyoongar *boodja*, Aboriginal resistance or even reconciliation. Fremantle's High Street reproductions generally work to reconnect the present with an imperial past and their place with the highest ground in London, St Paul's Cathedral.[27] These sacred-soliciting facades gesturing towards empire keep people on the straight and narrow-minded. After all, the 'shape of the thinkable future' depends on representations of the past and the present's relationship with the past.[28] Much has been invested in that past.

The Fremantle Society was established in 1972 to protect the city's built environment and other cultural heritage. The society, supported by the National Trust, has exercised considerable influence over the planning and imagining of Fremantle in recent years. The society's influence goes back to Gough Whitlam's Labor triumph in the 1972 federal election. This victory enabled the loyal Labor electorate of Fremantle to connect with a Federal Government introducing nation-building policies. Whitlam's new nationalism included heritage and environmental policies framed as the people's wishes against self-interested local business elites, multinational corporations and even state governments.[29] In a discourse of 'the people versus developers', the Whitlam government blamed degradation of the National Estate on the elevation of private over public interest, and established the link that poor people suffered most from the loss of parkland and familiar urban landscapes. This link strengthened the populism and ultimately the power of the national heritage project. Since the early 1970s, heritage funds for Fremantle have been directed towards memorialising the imperial/colonial contribution to nation building. Since 1971, the car parks have been removed from Kings Square and the sacred-soliciting geometry of High Street has become clearer. The aggressive reproduction of Fremantle's streetscape as a set of neoclassical facades signifying a glorious imperial – and increasingly nationalist – past has developed a certain expectation of architectural appropriateness within Fremantle community. To avoid transgression,[30] large architectural projects designed for Fremantle must fit in with this imperial/Australian past or at least gesture respectfully towards it.

On the evening of Saturday 16 May 2009, Adele Carles appeared jubilant at the party celebrating her victory in the Fremantle by-election. The Greens candidate had gained 54 per cent of votes on a two-party-preferred basis over Labor's Peter Tagliaferri.[31] Some analysts attributed this landslide win to changing demographics and the Liberal Party staying out of the contest. Locally, the *Fremantle Herald* put the result down to twenty years of disappointment with Labor, particularly its failure to stand against big radical property development. 'Port Coogee, ING on historic Victoria Quay, Three Harbours and now North Port Quay were the limit for many,' read an editorial.[32] 'Labor – the party that practically gave away hectares of sea bed at Coogee, earning developer Australand untold millions in profits – had become the party of the seedy and the greedy.'[33] The Greens had run a better campaign, been faster off the mark and more in touch with local sentiment. Meanwhile, Tagliaferri had suffered from awkward pre-selection, haunting council decisions and disastrous 'fence-sitting on North Port Quay'.[34]

Carles attributed her historic victory to the Greens policies in areas where Labor had failed to respond to people's concerns. Labor lost voters when it 'aligned with corporations and abandoned the environment', she said. 'We have attracted mainstream voters' giving her party the clear message that 'people want action', particularly against North Port Quay.[35] Lobbyists Anne Burns and John Halden tried to make the best of a bad result – for them and their client – in the media. Halden even told radio that, by his calculation, a majority of voters wanted the project.[36] But with an overwhelming 44 per cent of primary votes, Carles confidently responded that the former Labor politician couldn't do his maths: 'They made NPQ an election issue, but it backfired.' Gesturing towards Nik Varga's 3.5 per cent primary vote, Carles said: 'We now know there is not the support for NPQ.'[37]

Picking up the keys to Jim McGinty's old office, Carles began remaking her image as an incumbent rather than an opposition politician.[38] She would be inclusive and accepting of practical assistance, such as a friend moving in during the campaign to help her and Francois manage their household and care for the children. 'I don't agree with the superwoman image, it's damaging to women,' she said: 'I'll step up but will do this with a lot of support behind me.'[39]

Notes

1   K. Gelder & J. Jacobs, *Uncanny Australia: Sacredness and Identity in a Postcolonial Nation*, Melbourne University Press, Carlton South, 1998, p. 25.

2   P. J. Rich, *Elixir of Empire: The English Public Schools, Ritualism, Freemasonry, and Imperialism*, Regency Press, London, 1989, p. 18.

3   R. Loopers, *Fremantle Forever wins Australia Day award*, Freo's View, Fremantle, viewed 28 January 2014, <http://freoview.wordpress.

com/2014/01/27/21415/>.

4   *Officer (AO) in the General Division of the Order of Australia*, Governor-
     General of the Commonwealth of Australia, Canberra, viewed 28 January
     2014, <http://www.gg.gov.au/sites/default/files/files/honours/ad/
     Media%20Notes%20-%20AO%20%28final%29.pdf>.

5   D. Hutchison, *Fremantle Walks*, Fremantle Arts Centre Press, Fremantle,
     2006, p. 6.

6   T. Kerr, 'Reproducing temples in Fremantle', *International Journal of Heritage
     Studies*, vol. 18, no. 1, 2012, pp. 1–17.

7   R. Davidson & D. Davidson, *Fighting for Fremantle: the Fremantle Society
     Story*, Fremantle Society, Fremantle, 2010, pp. 36–157.

8   Gelder & Jacobs, *Uncanny Australia*, pp. 22–5.

9   G. Nowland, 'Fremantle: The port as a threshold of consciousness in the
     novel', *Westerly: a Quarterly Review*, no. 51, 2006, p. 147.

10   J. Stratton, 'Dying to come to Australia: Asylum seekers, tourists and death',
     in R. Summo-O'Connell (ed), *Imagined Australia: Reflections around the
     Reciprocal Construction of Identity between Australia and Europe*, Peter Lang,
     Bern, 2009, pp. 57–87.

11   J. White, 'Henry Reveley, architect and engineer', *Journal of the Royal
     Western Australia Historical Society*, vol. 7, no. 8, 1976, pp. 24–42.

12   N. Hudson-Rodd & G. A. Farrell, 'The Round House Gaol: Western
     Australia's first lunatic asylum', *Australia and New Zealand Journal of Mental
     Health Nursing*, vol. 7, no. 4, 1998, pp. 152–62.

13   S. Mickler, 'Curators and the colony: Managing the past at Rottnest Island
     Museum', *Continuum: The Australian Journal of Media & Culture*, vol. 3, no. 1,
     1990, pp. 84–100.

14   R. Scollon & S. W. Scollon, *Discourses in Place: Language in the Material World*,
     Routledge, London, 2003.

15   Victorian architecture, particularly its facades, was intended to be read like
     books containing abstract images of history in which representation of the
     Classic, for instance, was reduced to an essentialist pattern of pillar, base
     and arch. See E. N. Kaufman, 'Architectural representation in Victorian
     England', *Journal of the Society of Architectural Historians*, vol. 46, no. 1, 1987,
     pp. 30–38.

16   Freemasons played a major role in the production of Fremantle's
     streetscape. This is evident in the records of prominent people and
     buildings associated with Freemasonry in the Local History photographic
     collection of the Fremantle City Library. Also, see P. M. Brown, *The
     Merchant Princes of Fremantle: The Rise and Decline of a Colonial Elite
     1870–1900*, University of Western Australia Press, Nedlands, 1996.

17 J. S. Curl, *The Art and Architecture of Freemasonry: An Introductory Study*, Batsford, London, 1991, p. 117.

18 Ibid., p. 229.

19 *Welcome*, Flying Angel Club, Fremantle, 2010, viewed 29 January 2014, <http://www.flyingangel.org.au/>.

20 *King James Bible*, The Official King James Bible Online, viewed 29 January 2014, <http://www.kingjamesbibleonline. org/1611_Revelation-Chapter-11/>.

21 J. K. Ewers, *The Western Gateway: A History of Fremantle*, University of Western Australia Press, Nedlands, 1971, pp. 29–30.

22 Brown, *The Merchant Princes of Fremantle*, pp. 1–102.

23 M. Tull, *A Community Enterprise: The History of the Port of Fremantle, 1897 to 1997*, International Maritime Economic History Association, St. John's, 1997.

24 *Kings Square Architectural Competition 2013*, Tangelo Creative, City of Fremantle, Fremantle, 2013, viewed 29 January 2014, <http://kingssquare. fremantle.wa.gov.au/>.

25 Kelsall Binet Architects, *Monument Hill Memorial Reserve Fremantle Conservation Plan*, City of Fremantle, Fremantle, 2009, pp. 31–3.

26 Ibid.

27 This connection can be read in the dominant position of St Paul's Cathedral in the Pioneer Window of Fremantle's Church of St John the Evangelist. This window tells the story of emigration from England to Western Australia.

28 T. Bennett, *Birth of the Museum: History, Theory, Politics*, Routledge, London, 1995, p. 162.

29 Ibid., 143.

30 Scollon & Scollon, *Discourses in Place: Language in the Material World*, p. 149.

31 *ABC Elections*, Australian Broadcasting Corporation, Sydney, 2009, viewed 30 January 2014, <http://abc.net.au/elections/wa/2009/fremantle/>.

32 *Fremantle Herald*, 23 May 2009, p. 7.

33 Ibid.

34 Ibid.

35 *Fremantle Herald*, 23 May 2009, p. 3.

36 Ibid., p. 1.

37 Ibid., p. 3.

38 Ibid.

39 Ibid.

INVERSION

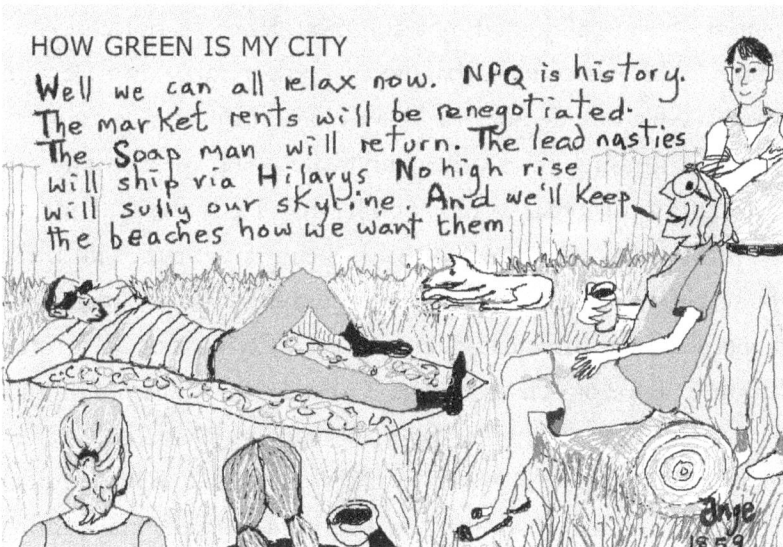

Courtesy of *Fremantle Herald*, 23 May 2009, page 4

'…*capital builds a geographical landscape in its own image at a certain point in time only to have to destroy it later in order to accommodate its own dynamic of endless capital accumulation, strong technological change, and fierce forms of class struggle*'.[1]

D. Harvey

'*Last Saturday the port said "enough!", showed Labor the door and shacked up with a new partner promising love and attention*'.[2]

A. Smith & B. Mitchell

On a winter's evening in 2009, an enthusiastic crowd poured into the parliament's gallery to peer down on Adele Carles as she prepared to address the Legislative Assembly for the first time. After acknowledging 'Nyoongah people as the traditional owners of this land', Carles attempted to alleviate any discomfort the old boys on blue benches may have felt about a Greens politician penetrating the chamber. As a mother first and environmentalist second, Carles promised cooperation through mutual interest: 'we are all joined by a common desire for our children's future'.[3] She maintained that people power made her election 'a victory for our democratic system'. Her campaign started out with less funding than other candidates, but voters wanted a community voice that would not sell out to big business. 'I am not the likeliest of candidates,' she said, 'being a woman with three young children.' She thanked her loving husband for 'rock-solid' support and her three daughters for 'the daily inspiration to keep standing up for our environment'. Carles also thanked her mother for courageously struggling 'to make ends meet as a sole parent without government support' in raising her and adopted brother Andrew, who 'had to face the cold reality of what it meant to be Aboriginal in this state. It meant being under suspicion and being subjected to overt racism'. On behalf of the Greens, Carles recognised Aboriginal 'sovereignty to the land known as the state of Western Australia' and apologised 'for their loss of country and for the injustices imposed on them'. She then reflected on her immediate failure as an MP to find crisis accommodation for a young Nyoongar man who had come to her office a week earlier desperately seeking a place to stay for the cold, damp night. Haunted by his image, she would 'work with this government to secure funding for additional crisis accommodation. It is inhumane' she said, in the wealthy state that 'hundreds of people sleep rough on the streets'. While the Nyoongar man was out of property and in the street, Nyoongar connection to place was in use for preserving colonial conditions of the street. Carles paid tribute to heritage campaigners for saving Fremantle's historic buildings then linked Indigenous notions of 'country' and Aboriginal learning with her mobilisation against coastal property developers. She took the legal argument for recognising Indigenous land rights and used it to recognise urban people's collective rights to spaces through an enduring connection to these spaces:

> I chose to stand up for South Beach because it is my country. I use the word "country" in the way that Aboriginal people have taught me. It is my place of belonging. It holds spiritual significance for me. I know many other people who feel like this about their beach.[4]

Her own love of a special place enabled empathy with other people's love of special places and 'to stand up for one special place is to begin the process of standing up for them all', said Carles, quoting Greens Senator Christine Milne: 'It is the beginning of becoming a global citizen'. Global citizens acted when governments failed to take 'responsibility for our environment' yet they were marginalised in being labelled 'activists'. Carles thanked people in Western Australia who had stood up for a special place or a variety of environmental ideals against the odds. She referred to people standing up against the threat of violence, arrest and legal cost orders from the timber industry to protect a native forest in Margaret River, then linked this to Fremantle community actions in which 'many of us unwittingly became campaigners as we saw our special places being threatened by inappropriate development'. When the Labor government approved the export of lead carbonate through Fremantle port, it was no 'wonder the North Port Quay consortium was under the illusion that anything goes' there. Yet the consortium's proposed radical change to coastal aesthetics had stimulated a conservative reaction, bringing this concerned mother of Fremantle into parliament. It supported their nostalgia for an idealised pace in an idealised place.[5] Emotionally sensitive, Carles was aware of the nostalgia sweeping through her electorate:

> I am lucky to own a home in Fremantle, because Fremantle is a very special place, as anyone who is fortunate enough to live there will tell you. I live at the south end in an old renovated cottage amongst neighbours who are like family. We all know each other in this part of town. People walk and cycle; children roam in and out of our homes. People rarely sell their houses here. They are not interested in bigger houses, the latest appliances or new cars. There are no lock-down garages or security gates to keep people out. We have our doors open so that people can come in. It is almost old-fashioned, and I would not trade that for the world. It is this sense of connection and desire to preserve what is special that sees Fremantle people being active citizens and politically engaged.[6]

Desire to preserve the beloved pace and place – to realise identity through restoration of desired experience – drove many voters to support Carles against the radical threat of North Port Quay. It did not matter that the project was proposed as a future sustainable-development solution to the global ecological threat of climate change when it meant an immediate threat to restoration of desired experience. It provoked the conservative reaction that spiralled antagonistically through the electoral process bringing Carles to office. Yet, insensitivity to such affect-driven passions seemed to have been lost in the rationalities of economic opportunism and ecological modernisation driving the project. Failure to account for such a probable conservative reaction suggests that the pursuit of capital accumulation requiring a radical, spatially engineered social change is not as rational as it seems.[7] Yet, insatiable desire for capital accumulation is just another passion; a subjectivity to sensual experience of objects. This passion is bound to be disrupted by other people's passions just as places are bound to be disrupted again and again by the coming to ground of new spaces of capital accumulation.[8] These mutually antagonistic relations in urban development arise when desire for accumulation collides with love of places. These relations are part of the process of capitalism. Greg Poland needed a new space for accumulation, and he thought he could legitimise its imposition by promoting North Port Quay as 'the world's first carbon-free development'.[9] Imposition of this radical spatial change over beloved places antagonised local people. Radical change met conservative response.

Adele Carles wanted to conserve place relations. She was not against business. She was faithful to liberalism, at least the Amsterdam variety.[10] Business should be involved with community and government in strategically planning Fremantle as a 'residential port' that prioritised health and safety.[11] Like Professor Newman, Carles believed in the ecological threats of oil-resource limits and climate change and the catastrophic consequences of sea-level rises, species extinction and people's dislocation. Carles argued that government could solve these problems through policy and legislation, by adopting renewable energy production and blocking new coal-fired power stations. Government inaction on this could not be justified, said Carles: 'imagine trying to justify it to a child, a child who is now learning about global warming'.[12] Departing from Newman, Carles called for the retention of institutionalised democratic participation in environmental-policy making, for preservation of coastal commons and for people's participation in modernisation. Carles argued that ecological modernisation should be for the sakes of 'our children'; apparently not the consumers in North Port Quay advertising. 'We must rise to the challenge of transforming our polluting energy industry into a clean industry,' she said. 'Renewable energy is free once we have the infrastructure in place because no corporation can own the sun or the wind.' She called this 'the smart way forward and it is the ethical way forward. We Greens like to ask: In 50 years' time, will our children be looking back at us smiling?'[13] This was Carles' greatest moment as a public figure after years of hard-fought campaigning against coastal property development. The road to popular appeal was laid with traps and hardship, sang Fremantle's more famous brunette in AC/DC's 'Long way to the top'. And like Bon Scott, burnt and buried in Fremantle,[14] Carles would end her rise with a spectacular fall.

In February 2010, on the eve of the thirtieth anniversary of Scott's 'death by misadventure'[15] after a big night out in London, Carles would emerge from an Albany motel room with Liberal Treasurer Troy Buswell.[16] As rumours of this unlikely affair began to emerge, Carles put her side of the story first to *The Sunday Times*: 'I could attempt to portray myself as the vulnerable one who was taken advantage of,' she said, pictured in red on the Whalers Tunnel entrance backgrounded by High Street heritage.[17] 'However, this is simply not true. We made a mutual, albeit stupid, decision as two consenting adults'.[18] Carles smiled endearingly to the camera, like Scott performing 'Highway to Hell':

livin' easy
lovin' free
season ticket on a one way ride
askin' nothin'
leave me be
takin' everythin' in my stride
don't need reason
don't need rhyme
ain't nothin' that I'd rather do…
I'm on the highway to hell…[19]

Carles apologised to Fremantle constituents and promised to end the affair. Buswell admitted to using a government car and taxpayer-funded accommodation to meet his lover[20] apologised to both families then later resigned as Treasurer.[21] The Greens promised to stick by Carles, but she soon resigned citing insufficient support from Greens MP Giz Watson and other party members.[22] Carles' resignation was a blow to the Greens, said Watson, putting her decision down to overwhelming emotion.[23] Free of the Greens affiliation, Carles focused on her relationship with Buswell and Liberal-party politics. She gave this undertaking in the hope of getting more staff and resources for her constituency office, but was betrayed by Barnett who mocked her promise in the national press.[24] After associating with Buswell, splitting from the Greens and being betrayed by the Liberal premier, it seemed that things could get no worse for Carles, the politician. However, a public break up with Buswell in 2012 and his subsequent defamation action would damage her electoral image beyond repair. Buswell sued Carles for saying she had ended their relationship after the then-housing-minister 'dry humped' the managing director of Kailis Bros at a party of Perth's moneymen, at the Peppermint

Grove home of property magnate Nigel Satterley.[25] Carles found herself up against the 'mates' club of Perth's political, media and business elites. Rather than seeing a problem in the silencing of Carles and what she, potentially, could have told the public about these elites, media focused on blaming Carles, not Buswell, for the affair.[26] At the next election, Barnett's government was returned to power with Buswell coming back into the position of Treasurer; his clever-bloke image restored. Meanwhile, Fremantle voters ditched Carles in favour of a return to Labor in the form of union-secretary Simone McGurk. Despite Carles' consistent position against reclamation at Rous Head while representing Fremantle, voters seemed more concerned about her apparent inconsistency with the ideal Fremantle mother image that had been publicised during the campaign against North Port Quay. The swing against Carles was predictable yet shattering, from 44 per cent of the primary vote in 2009[27] to just 5 per cent in 2013.[28] She was well behind Labor, Liberal and the Greens' new candidate, Andrew Sullivan.

But before these compounding public scandals ruined Carles' promising political career, North Port Quay would be banished from Fremantle and the Greens would take control of Town Hall. The powerful conservative movement against radical spatial change would still have its day.

Notes

1   D. Harvey, *Spaces of Hope*, Edinburgh University Press, Edinburgh, 2000, p. 177.
2   *Fremantle Herald*, 23 May 2009, p. 1.
3   WA Parliament Hansard, 9 June 2009.
4   Ibid.
5   S. Boym, 'Nostalgia and its discontents', *The Hedgehog Review*, Summer, 2007, pp. 7–18.

6   WA Parliament Hansard, 9 June 2009.
7   The irrationality of capitalist logic could be sensed through engagement with interactive displays at the *Slave Trade: The Dark Chapter* exhibition at the Scheepvaart Museum in Amsterdam in 2013. The exhibition, adapted from Leo Balai's research on the sinking of the slave ship *Leusden*, unsettles visitors by engaging them in support of the capitalist logic of slavery after showing them the immensely irrational damage it does to people. The exhibition suggests that we moderns fail to act ethically because we do not understand our mind's association of affects, an understanding called for in Spinoza's writing on ethics at the beginning of the Enlightenment. See L. Balai, *Het Slavenschip* Leusden: *Slavenschepen en de West Indische Compagnie, 1720–1738*, Walberg Pers, Zutphen, 2011. Also see S. Nadler, *Spinoza's Ethics: An Introduction*, Cambridge University Press, Cambridge, 2006.
8   Harvey, *Spaces of Hope*, pp. 159–73.
9   *Fremantle Herald*, 14 June 2008, p. 7.
10 R. Shorto, *Amsterdam: A History of the World's Most Liberal City*, Little, Brown, London, 2014.
11 WA Parliament Hansard, 9 June 2009.
12 Ibid.
13 Ibid.
14 C. Walker, *Highway to Hell: The Life and Death of AC/DC Legend Bon Scott*, Verse Chorus Press, Portland, 2007.
15 Ibid., p. 260.
16 A. Burrell, 'Just another sordid notch in the WA bedpost', *The Australian*, 1 May 2010, viewed 6 February 2014, <http://www.theaustralian.com.au/opinion/just-another-sordid-notch-in-the-wa-bedpost/story-e6frg6zo-1225860473179>.
17 J. Spagnolo, 'Greens MP Adele Carles confesses to secret affair with Troy Buswell', *PerthNow*, 24 April 2010, viewed 6 February 2014, <http://www.perthnow.com.au/news/greens-mp-adele-carles-confesses-to-secret-affair-with-troy-buswell/story-e6frg12c-1225857829924>.
18 Ibid.
19 A. Young, M. Young & B. Scott, 'Highway to Hell', Sony Music Entertainment, 2013, viewed 10 February 2014, <http://www.acdc.com/us/music/bonfire/highway-hell>.
20 M. Colvin, 'WA Treasurer confirms affair with Greens MP', *ABC News*, 26 April 2010, viewed 6 February 2014, <http://www.abc.net.au/pm/content/2010/s2883022.htm>.
21 C. Sonti, L. Phillips and J. Sapienza, 'Buswell resigns over secret sex sessions

on taxpayers' tab,' *PerthNow*, 24 April 2010, viewed 6 February 2014, <http://www.watoday.com.au/wa-news/buswell-resigns-over-secret-sex-sessions-on-taxpayers-tab-20100425-tksk.html>.

22 L. Jones, 'Greens party reject they bullied Carles into admitting affair', *PerthNow*, 7 May 2010, viewed 6 February 2014, <http://www.perthnow.com.au/news/western-australia/greens-party-reject-they-bullied-carles-into-admitting-affair/story-e6frg13u-1225863805158>.

23 Ibid.

24 P. Taylor, 'Colin Barnett says independent MP promised complete support', *The Australian*, 9 November 2010, viewed 6 February 2014, <http://www.theaustralian.com.au/national-affairs/state-politics/colin-barnett-says-independent-mp-promised-complete-support/story-e6frgczx-1225949645334>.

25 J. Spanolo, 'Troy Buswell recommends top job for 'dry hump' witness', *The Australian*, 22 December 2012, viewed 6 February 2014, <http://www.theaustralian.com.au/news/top-job-for-dry-hump-witness/story-e6frg6n6-1226542425962>.

26 *The West Australian*, 13 December 2012, p. 21.

27 Ibid.

28 Western Australian Electoral Commission, Perth, 2013, viewed 6 February 2014, <http://www.elections.wa.gov.au/elections/state/sg2013/la/FRE>.

TIME KEEPING

Photograph by author

'Go forwards not backwards.'

John Alberti

'I mean it's just ludicrous, absolutely ludicrous. It would be the destruction not the salvation of Fremantle.'[1]

Les Lauder

Fremantle Town Hall is a most impressive time-keeping piece if approached from the west end of High Street. At the base of the building's clock tower, great wooden doors within a limestone porch suggest something solemn going on inside. The interior is used mostly for banquets and quirky exhibitions these days, but an interesting town-hall debate may still be held there. Most municipal debate goes on behind this building in the council chambers of the Town Hall Centre annex, facing William Street. To follow the council's evening meetings, constituents must enter the annex via a set of external stairs opposite the old Myer's block. Inside, council meetings are held in a white-walled theatre. Councillors and administrators sit on three sides of a square while the public and press may form a dislocated fourth side on rows of (typically empty) seats.

At the council's monthly meeting on 24 June 2009, Deputy Mayor John Dowson introduced a motion to reject North Port Quay. Dowson was chairing this meeting in Peter Tagliaferri's absence. The former history teacher and champion of Fremantle's mercantile heritage set out to put the city's rejection of North Port Quay on public record. Dowson's strategy was to discredit the project first by having a crack at its spin doctor, John Halden. Dowson asked whether the Southern Metropolitan Regional Council (SMRC) had paid '$120,000 to lobbyist John Halden's company for public relations work?'[2] Halden Burns had been paid a $5,000 monthly retainer in 2007 and 2008 by the SMRC for strategic communications advice in managing the unpopular stench around its recycling facility. Dowson then proceeded to ask a question that associated this consultancy with Halden's work for North Port Quay and an 'infamous' event that had ended Halden's parliamentary career.

Later in the meeting, Dowson introduced his motion to reject North Port Quay on the grounds that the issue was distracting council when it needed a clear position in the state government's consideration of the future of Fremantle port. The North Port

Quay concept should be rejected, Dowson said, because on top of the project's environmental claims being misleading; even 'a five-year-old can see' it would not work on environmental grounds.[3]

In response, gruff Greens councillor Jon Strachan stood briefly, said abruptly: 'You haven't convinced me. I'll move a deferral.'[4] 'No!' cried a shocked audience member before ducking in embarrassment, covering mouth and emotion in hands.[5] Strachan explained his surprising position. 'I'll put on public record now that I am no supporter of North Port Quay,' he said, 'but we must ensure that any motion of no support would withstand public criticism and modifications to the proposal. I want our planning officers to write a report to us that…looks at the planning grounds, the sustainability issues, the social justice issues,' he said. 'Just to say that we don't support North Port Quay is really not robust enough.'[6] Councillor Bill Massie supported Strachan's motion for the council to defer its rejection of North Port Quay, but for quite different reasons. 'I actually support the development and I'm quite happy to tell people I do,'[7] Massie said emphatically in thick Scottish accent. He called for a debate in the chambers with councillor Pettitt and fellow representatives of Murdoch University on one side and North Port Quay developers on the other. This would be better than fearing the future, said the local real-estate agent. 'We are still sitting here in Fremantle in our little egg box not prepared to move on,' Massie said emphatically, 'it is a great proposal, I believe, and not the first time in the world to reclaim some water.'[8]

Councillor Les Lauder stood up to Massie, arguing that a debate would be a waste of time since voters had made their opposition to the project known in the by-election. The beret-wearing defender of High Street heritage argued that council should reject North Port Quay on principle without waiting for a Planning Services

Committee report. The electorate had 'overwhelmingly rejected the idea' of North Port Quay in the Fremantle by-election, he said.[9] 'This is simply a speculative project to make a lot of money. It's dressing itself up, in this rather flimsy cloak by using terms such as sustainability', which Lauder said was ludicrous given the amount of land available in Western Australia. He posited that the project was about selling very expensive housing units over the ocean, and 'at least half of them would be bought by overseas, eh, people. Nothing wrong with that in itself, but this isn't something for the Fremantle community at all'. The founding president of the Fremantle Society argued that Strachan's deferral for the preparation of a report would 'waste our overworked planning department's staff's time' on something 'the community has shown it doesn't want...we have to stand for principle and the principle is clear. Nobody apart from the odd odd person...'[10] Lauder was interrupted by laughter over this apparent reference to the few North Port Quay supporters on council. Councillor John Alberti interjected over this reference then alleged that Lauder had a hypocritical self-interested position on heritage protection and property development in Fremantle.

> *20:59:18 John Alberti:* Get a life Councillor Lauder, get a life.
> *20:59:19 Les Lauder:* If, if you want to...make a decision on the basis of what the community thinks
> *20:59:25 John Alberti:* Go forwards not backwards.
> *20:59:28 Les Lauder:* ...let's have a referendum if you want to do that. But we have to stand for something. And...the public has told us very clearly that...the public doesn't want this, why waste time on reports and so forth when it's so obviously alien to Fremantle's

interest? How on Earth would you get 20,000 people, one assumes with cars, through North Fremantle for one thing? I mean, if you just start thinking about it… it's just not what Fremantle wants. Certainly we've got large areas of Fremantle that we can and will redevelop, but Fremantle's future doesn't depend on a speculative project stuck out in the ocean that will probably be washed away in the first major storm we get. Let's not even think about the…carbon footprint that's going to stomp on this area if such a thing's built. I mean it's just ludicrous, absolutely ludicrous. It would be the destruction not the salvation of Fremantle. It would be the destruction of Fremantle. It's nonsense and I support this recommendation.

21:00:37 Les Lauder sits. John Alberti raises hand.

21:00:40 John Dowson: Councillor Alberti.

21:00:41 John Alberti stands.

21:00:42 John Alberti: I think Councillor Lauder got it all wrong, actually. He says the community and doesn't want it. That's only a minority that wants it, eh, doesn't want it. You know, how many people have you actually spoken to that actually want it. You know you remind of a grumpy old man, you remind me,

21:00:58 John Dowson: Excuse me councillor, Councillor Alberti![11]

This exchange made page 2 of *Fremantle Herald* under the header: 'NPQ debate turns nasty'.[12] The same edition carried a letter by Peter Newman arguing that Dowson should not so readily dismiss North Port Quay as 'unsustainable' because it is 'less car-based than urban fringe development' and it 'demonstrates the next generation of carbon-free technologies in city building'.[13] Newman argued that no-one at a recent sustainability conference in Canada and other events away from Fremantle objected to the project being presented as an example of sustainability.

Back inside the council chambers, Councillor Alberti argued in support of deferring the motion to reject North Port Quay on the basis of it being a good project that would bring 'good revenue to the city of Fremantle'.[14] Councillor Pettitt also supported the deferral, but for reasons similar to Strachan's. Pettitt waved his hands and mumbled, 'there is such a lack of a gain, making decisions in a vacuum. Along with you Mr Dowson I think on principle I'm not going to be supporting this development.'[15] Then Councillor Robert Fittock stood firmly for North Port Quay and the deferral to give its consortium a chance to state its case through community consultation. Otherwise, he said, we are 'sending a very clear message to those people, the owners, developers, investors: Don't do anything visionary in Fremantle – we don't want it'.[16]

Before calling for a vote, Deputy Mayor Dowson tried to persuade councillors not to support the deferral of his motion to reject North Port Quay. 'It's ridiculous to think that we would ask our officers to go off and be distracted from their hugely impor-tant and busy lives to write a report on a concept,'[17] he said from his seat. 'How can they sit down and examine the environmental credentials or the transport linkages or any of the issues, the major issues, for something that is purely a concept?' Hand moving vertically in emphatic motion with speech, Dowson continued: 'This is not a development proposal by someone who has given us a fee and wants us to examine something. It's an idea floating around by a group of businessmen,' he said. 'The government, the present premier and the previous premier have made it very clear that they don't want to waste time on it and we shouldn't be [wasting] time on it.'[18] To this, Councillor Fittock asked if the deputy mayor was aware 'the government is waiting for the report from the Port optimum planning group before deciding its position on North Port Quay.'[19] Dowson acknowledged the factual basis of this rhetorical question then heard from Strachan, perhaps regrettably, in closing the discussion around his motion. Strachan said the council had fallen into the trap of having to consider North Port Quay thanks to Dowson. 'We could have just ignored it and hoped it would go away. But you have brought a notice,' Strachan said, so they were obliged 'to go through the process of explaining why we are rejecting it'.[20] A deferral would allow the planning officers to write a report 'which gives good reason for our decision. Otherwise we sound like spoilt children saying *I don't want it*.'

21:08:59: John Dowson: OK, thank you councillors. Those in favour of the deferral

21:09:02 Les Lauder: Can I just say…

21:09:02 Jon Strachan raises hand and Les Lauder stands.

21:09:03 Les Lauder: Can I just ask a question, deputy mayor, members, do you have any idea how much it would cost to make a detailed analysis of this proposal?

21:09:13 Jon Strachan: (words unclear).

21:09:17 Les Lauder: …I mean it's a rhetorical question but I can tell you it would be enormous amount of time if the officers were doing it themselves

21:09:26 Jon Strachan: (words unclear).

21:08:28: John Dowson: Excuse me Councillor Strachan I'm in charge of the meeting. Thank you, councillor.

21:09:30 Jon Strachan: Then get in charge of it please.

21:09:32: Voices from unclear sources: Excuse me. Fair enough.

21:09:40: John Dowson: Thank you councillors. All right, all those in favour of the deferral

21:09:43: Hands raised by John Alberti, Robert Fittock, Donna Haney, Shirley Mackay, Bill Massie, Brad Pettitt and Jon Strachan.

21:09:43: John Dowson: Those against.

21:09:44: Hands raised by John Dowson, Georgie Adeane and Les Lauder.

21:09:47: John Dowson: OK, the deferral is carried.[21]

The council's Planning Services Committee asked the municipality's manager for planning projects to report on North Port Quay. Three months later the committee received the report, which raised significant concerns about the project's environmental impacts, compatibility with Fremantle Port, traffic generation and detrimental impact on employment in Fremantle's city centre.[22] To which, Les Lauder reportedly quipped: 'It's the longest way of stating the bleeding obvious I have ever seen'.[23] At last Peter Tagliaferri took a position on North Port Quay, moving that the committee report these concerns about North Port Quay to council. His motion was supported in the committee by Dowson, Fittock, Lauder and Strachan, but opposed by Alberti and Massie.[24] Immediately, Dowson moved the committee recommendation that Fremantle Council should 'express its strong opposition to the North Port Quay concept' for its incompatibility with port operations.[25] The committee also recommended that council should reject North Port Quay's concept of reclaiming the ocean off Rous Head for housing due to environmental and transport concerns, and that it should advise project proponents and relevant state ministers of the council's position. This motion was supported by all committee members except Alberti and Massie.[26] The *Fremantle Herald* reported the 'council staff report' had given North Port Quay 'the thumbs down' on the grounds of publicly available information after proponents had ignored their requests for data'.[27] This news spoke to a greater story about 'the Barnett government's plans to strip elected councils of planning powers and hand them to minister-appointed "experts"'.[28] This plan, which became public in September, would reduce council authority to approving only minor projects. Retiring mayor Tagliaferri said, 'we may as well pack our bags and go'.[29] Such a change would also work against the importance of local press:

> WA planning minister John Day's proposal is the latest in a chain of moves that have long diluted local planning authority.
>
> Already, most decisions by elected councils are subject to being overturned at the whim of the powerful, unelected State Administrative Tribunal.
>
> Mr Day now wants to introduce another layer of panels – each consisting of three unelected experts and two local councillors – over the top of councils.
>
> Council staff will still do the legwork, but decisions on projects worth $2m or more will rest with the panels...[30]

Developers, but not discontent locals, could appeal a panel decision and Mr Day would give himself more power to intervene on significant projects.[31] The changes were reportedly 'cooked up in Canberra between public service mandarins, politicians and the development industry'.[32] The reforms, already introduced in other Australian states, supported rapid approval of major projects while 'stopping locals from putting political pressure on councillors about projects they don't want in their community'.[33] Still in the good books, Carles called the proposed changes undemocratic: 'With no third-party appeal rights in WA and political donations influencing planning, this unelected panel could become a developers' rubber stamp.'[34] This would be an issue for the upcoming council election. Brad Pettitt was in campaign mode for the mayoral position: 'Fremantle people and council must have the right to say what kind of development should happen in Fremantle.'[35] Fellow Greens member and rival for the position Jon Strachan said councils should have more rather than less authority to reduce state red tape and speed up development. A third Greens member in the mayoral race, Michael Martin, who had made his name campaigning against coastal mega development, said the change would lead to decisions that were 'out of touch with local community sentiment'.[36] From its quaint editorial office in Cliff Street, the rooster squawked red ink: 'if the changes had been in place in recent years both the North Port Quay and the Three Harbours Project might conceivably have been approved while the campaign to reserve 17 hectares of parkland at Leighton Beach would never have got off the ground'.[37]

A week later, on 23 September, Fremantle Council moved to support the Fremantle Planning Committee's concerns about North Port Quay.[38] The council also endorsed Dowson's motion to reject the project and tell the world about it. The motion against North Port Quay was carried with nine votes in favour and only Fittock, Alberti and Massie against it.[39]

Notes

1   Transcript of Fremantle Council meeting on 24 June 2009. See Appendix 004 in T. Kerr, 'Representing ecological threats and negotiating green built environment', PhD thesis, Curtin University, 2012.
2   Ibid.
3   Ibid.
4   Ibid.
5   Ibid.
6   Ibid.
7   Ibid.
8   Ibid.
9   Ibid.
10 Ibid.
11 Ibid.
12 *Fremantle Herald*, 27 June 2009, p. 2.
13 Ibid., p. 6.
14 Transcript of Fremantle Council meeting on 24 June, 2009. See Appendix 004 in T. Kerr, 'Representing ecological threats and negotiating green built environment'.
15 Ibid.
16 Ibid.
17 Ibid.
18 Ibid.
19 Ibid.
20 Ibid.
21 Ibid.
22 City of Fremantle, *Agenda – Ordinary Meeting of Council: 23 September 2009*, City of Fremantle, Fremantle, 2009.
23 *Fremantle Herald*, 19 September 2009, p. 2.
24 City of Fremantle, *Agenda – Ordinary Meeting of Council: 23 September 2009*, p. 80.
25 Ibid., p. 81.
26 Ibid., p. 82.
27 *Fremantle Herald*, 19 September 2009, p. 2.
28 Ibid., p. 1.
29 Ibid.
30 Ibid., pp. 1–3.
31 Ibid., p. 3.
32 Ibid.
33 Ibid.

34 Ibid.
35 Ibid.
36 Ibid.
37 Ibid.
38 City of Fremantle, *Minutes – Ordinary Meeting of Council: 23 September 2009*, City of Fremantle, Fremantle, 2009.
39 Ibid., p. 87.

GREENS COUNCIL

Courtesy of *The West Australian*, 17 October 2009, page 32

'North Port Quay is a classic example of where the term 'sustainable development' has been usurped by people who are using it as a form of gloss, intending to make us feel good.'[1]

Michael Martin

'We should be playing the ball not the person.'[2]

Brad Pettitt

Brad Pettitt cycled his way into Fremantle's mayoral office in October 2009. The Associate Professor at Murdoch University had appeared again and again in the press in 2008 and 2009 as a cycling sustainability mover and shaker. He typically appeared pictured in hip downtown settings, cycling in office attire against backdrops such as the graffitied Wool Stores skating ledge in Fremantle.[3] Pettitt was a genius at appearing with bricolage suggesting an engaging sustainable city, something lacking in North Port Quay's publicity department. Pettitt also made himself helpful and accessible to constituents. He could be found on Thursday evenings negotiating constituent demands among the eclectic mix of plants and furniture at X-Wray cafe, bicycles parked out front opposite Fremantle's art-house cinema. A dedicated, youthful team of volunteers assembled around Pettitt seeking to practise and prophesise a more engaged form of urban environmental sustainability for Fremantle. It helped that the uncool North Port Quay lurked on the horizon. In comparison, Pettitt's vision of an environmentally sustainable Fremantle seemed positively engaging, appealing and doable. Standing against the NPQ project became the cornerstone policy of Brad Pettitt's mayoral campaign, 'Doing it different'.[4] Besides a devoted following, Pettitt was aided by a storm that tore chunks out of South Beach in the winter of 2009. As storm damage became front-page news,[5] Pettitt advised locals 'to be extremely cautious with proposed island developments like NPQ' as they could wreck the beaches in the same way that the locally maligned Port Coogee project had interrupted 'the natural movement and replenishment of sand on our beaches'.[6] Pettitt saw that standing for 'our beaches' against coastal development had worked in the election campaigns of fellow party members. This beach damage was a glimpse of things coming to Fremantle when climate change was exacerbated by coastal property development, he said in the dual roles of councillor and head of Murdoch University's Sustainability unit.[7]

Pettitt was on his way to victory in the mayoral race even before his intention to run was announced in the press on the day

of the Fremantle by-election.[8] He reportedly made the announcement early so that his decision would not be seen as exploiting a
by-election result against Mayor Tagliaferri. Pettitt wanted to be
the 'mayor who could work with all sides of the political spectrum
and overcome the divisions that have plagued council'.[9] Pictured
with sleeves rolled up ready for business in the *Fremantle Herald,* he
was described in this report:

> At 36 Cr Pettitt is the only Generation Xer on council
> and is behind the Fremantle Network, a think-tank of
> young Freo people whom he hopes will become the
> nucleus of the port city's next wave of community and
> business leaders.
>
> Amongst the network's projects is developing
> "innovative" policies on affordable housing, "so people
> like teachers and nurses can afford to both live and work
> in Freo".
>
> As Dr Pettitt he heads Murdoch University's sus-
> tainability school and is highly critical of the North Port
> Quay project, spruiked by his former boss and mentor
> Peter Newman…[10]

By July, the Greens had three parliamentary members working
out of offices in Fremantle: Adele Carles and Lynn MacLaren
in state parliament and Scott Ludlam in the Australian Senate.
Liberal parliamentary representation had been washed out of
the city and Labor representation had been whittled down to
the federal member Melissa Clarke.[11] MacLaren had just joined
parliament again, criticising North Port Quay in her inaugural
speech. The topic remained hot, although the consortium had
given up advertising. While standing firm against the project,

Pettitt offered a more conciliatory tone towards its proponents: they should play the ball, not the man. For an ambitious future mayor, it was not nice to see fellow public figures held to popular account in Fremantle. In one of his many opinion articles, Pettitt said he was not proud that debate around North Port Quay in the by-election had been dominated by character attacks.[12] While not supporting the project, he maintained an interest in the ideas integral to it. These were the 'focus of my conversations with Professor Peter Newman, a long-time colleague and friend, who for decades has worked on making human settlements more sustainable'. Rather than see debate 'sidelined by negative conjecture about its supporters', it would have 'been more productive to focus the debate on how we might bring the sustainability elements of NPQ to shore and into new developments in Fremantle'.[13] The campaign questions raised by Pettitt indicate that he shared Newman's belief that new property development was needed in Fremantle but that it should complement the city's heritage. Six weeks before the mayoral election, Pettitt appeared merrily on a bicycle leading dozens of other cyclists up an urban street in a photograph published by *Fremantle Herald* alongside an opinion article by him. Confident of victory, Pettitt set out to calm the storm of populism produced in reaction to North Port Quay and to protect the reputations of councillors supporting other forms of property development:

> I hope in the coming months that mayoral and council candidates can have these debates with the broader community without worrying that if they dare have a view they will be subject to negative vitriol and have their integrity questioned.

164

As we leave one election behind and prepare for another in October it is worth considering that how we behave in these elections reflects on what kind of community we want to be and what kind of council we want to have.

I want to be part of a community that proudly has robust debate over important issues but in doing so encourages and respects a diversity of views. It is worth remembering that often those who engage in negative personal attacks do so because they do not have a positive vision for the future. And it is a positive vision that Freo desperately needs right now.[14]

Brad Pettitt structured his mayoral election campaign on an alternative green-city concept that included an appreciation of Fremantle's existing built environment and a vision to protect its 'economic and social heritage'.[15] Pettitt argued extensively in favour of new property development in Fremantle on the basis that the city had stagnated and was no longer considered an important urban centre by state planners. He argued that a 'bold vision' for Fremantle would be required to overcome threats to Fremantle's social heritage and economic heritage. Pettitt argued that Fremantle community had protected its past and, now, it was time to protect its future by 'saying "yes" to substantial new developments that are compatible with our historical strengths'.[16] North Port Quay was inappropriate and 'overblown', he said, whereas any 'new development should be the heritage of the future; high quality, mixed use, environmentally sustainable, diverse and adaptable'.[17] Pettitt's campaign called for action in Fremantle by 'an engaged community'.[18] Meanwhile, fellow Green Jon Strachan advertised his mayoral ambition in terms of bringing about 'a strong independent Fremantle' based on accountable, progressive governance that built on past strengths and secured Fremantle's future.[19] A few weeks later Strachan shifted his focus to reviving community engagement, Fremantle's cultural and built heritage and its regional status.[20] But his advertisement and ideas seemed small compared to Pettitt's and miniature against Michael Martin's half-page advertisement. Among red and blue horizontal stripes, Martin offered himself as a 'better kind of mayor' who had 'led the successful campaign to protect Fremantle's beaches' from the Three Harbours development.[21] He also advertised extensive experience in social policy and relationship building.[22] Les Lauder took out a full-page advertisement in the *Fremantle Herald* endorsing Martin on the grounds that his 'successful leadership of the Save Freo Beaches Alliance inspired thousands in the community and brought change to Fremantle politics'.[23] The advertisement, advising readers to think carefully before voting, lamented Brad Pettitt's performance on Fremantle Council and implied he may secretly favour North Port Quay:

> John Dowson moved to reject the concept but Crs Pettitt and Strachan strangely voted to get the city's planners to do a report on it. Such a report can have no meaning. Cr Pettitt said there were good elements in NPQ.[24]

Lauder's advertisement suggested that candidates failing to absolutely condemn North Port Quay would be doomed in the election. Yet Pettitt was unstoppable with the *Fremantle Herald* at his back. 'Pettitt tops poll' read a headline on the newspaper's *vox populi* survey. Pettitt was endorsed ahead of other candidates for his environmental credentials and for having a better vision for Fremantle.[25] The newspaper ran an opinion piece, 'A process of elimination', by Roy Lewisson, endorsing Brad Pettitt as the best of six candidates for mayor because he had been an excellent councillor and a successful Dean of Sustainability at Murdoch University bringing environmental progress in the city:[26]

> Fremantle is now a national leader in sustainability and in addressing this century's biggest challenge – climate change. Brad has strongly represented the community by opposing issues such as NPQ and the new High Street that obliterate the golf course. But he can work equally well with the business sector to make sure Fremantle remains a city that still has decent shops and jobs.[27]

Lewisson quickly dismissed Martin as a candidate because he had not served the community on council. He said 'this would seem a somewhat fundamental criteria, if for no other reason than to understand the workings, procedures, policies, proto-cols, committee structures and some of the more subtle council manoeuvres'. The council's precinct contact for White Gum Valley called on Martin to run for council instead: 'You appear to have the makings of a fine councillor'.[28] Lewisson's article suggested a two-horse race between Brad Pettitt and Jon Strachan, but it was only ever an unequal race between the two candidates most widely known to oppose coastal development. That is, Pettitt and Martin. And this lopsided competition became personal, with Martin accusing Pettitt of unfair advantage in the Great 2009 Freo Mayoral Debate held at the Fremantle Town Hall on the evening of 22 September. From opposite sides of the hall's wooden stage, Martin blindsided Pettitt with the accusation that he had access to constituent questions sent by email to debate organisers before this popular event,[29] which was hosted by the University of Notre Dame, Fremantle Chamber of Commerce, Fremantle Society and Fremantle Network.[30] In this tense exchange, Pettitt leapt to his feet and fervently denied that he could still access the email account used to solicit public questions. Much of the audience was with Pettitt, booing Martin for attempting to denigrate their ideal man for mayor. When the debate got underway, Strachan was the only candidate to express opposition to North Port Quay and building over the sea in the opening statement. However, when the question of this project was put to candidates later in the debate, five were clearly against North Port Quay while one remained ambivalent. Pettitt said he was opposed from the outset although the project had good elements that could be adopted onshore for carbon-neutral development in Fremantle's East End. Martin stood opposed to North Port Quay along with any reclamation of the seabed. Shirley Mackay said it was an 'absolute no no'.[31] Sandro Brignoli said it was a beautiful project but nonsensical due to rising sea levels. The one dissenting voice, former councillor Phil Douglas, said he reserved the right not to pass judgement until a development application had come before council.

Coming into the election, Pettitt was clearly out in front of all the other candidates in the cafes, on his bike, and in the press. On election day, 17 October, *The West Australian* had him positioned as the candidate most able to stop Fremantle slipping further behind Perth as an urban centre.[32] Pettitt was the candidate 'pushing for change' so that Fremantle would become 'a real lively centre where you would work, live and shop'.[33] As though he were already mayor, Pettitt talked to the press about the real challenge of taking these 'bones of a great city' and building on them and 'to make sure it is not just a museum town of old buildings and places where you go and buy an ice-cream and a coffee'.[34]

The issue of North Port Quay drifted into the background where Michael Martin still spoke out against it as a form of 'sustainable development' that had been 'usurped by people who are using it as a form of gloss, intending to make us feel good'.[35]

Brad Pettitt was declared mayor on 19 October with 46 per cent of 8,226 valid votes. Trailing him by a long way was Martin with 16 per cent of the vote, McKay with 14 per cent, Douglas with 12 per cent, Strachan with 10 per cent and Brignoli with just 3 per cent.[36] This change in mayor marked the end of public discussion of North Port Quay as Pettitt embarked on the quest of bringing a more engaging form of sustainable development to Fremantle to complement its colonial heritage.

Pettitt has claimed many achievements as mayor since 2009, bringing almost $1 billion of investment plans to Fremantle while remaining accessible to its constituents. 'For more information, please read my blog,' he says.[37]

Notes

1   *The West Australian,* 17 October 2009, p. 32.
2   *Fremantle Herald,* 4 July 2009, p. 5.
3   *The West Australian,* 17 October 2009, p. 32.
4   *Policy – North Port Quay (NPQ),* 8 August 2009, B. Pettitt, Fremantle, viewed 9 September 2009, <http://www.bradpettitt.org/?page_id=93>.
5   *Fremantle Herald,* 4 July 2009, p. 1.
6   Ibid., p. 27.
7   Ibid.
8   *Fremantle Herald,* 16 May 2009, p. 3.
9   Ibid.
10 Ibid.
11 *Fremantle Herald,* 4 July 2009, p. 11.
12 Ibid., p. 5.
13 Ibid.
14 Ibid.
15 *Fremantle Herald,* 5 September 2009, p. 5.
16 Ibid.

17 Ibid.
18 *Fremantle Herald*, 19 September 2009, p. 3.
19 Ibid.
20 Ibid., p. 5.
21 Ibid.
22 Ibid.
23 Ibid., p. 7.
24 Ibid.
25 Ibid., p. 11.
26 Ibid., p. 5.
27 Ibid.
28 Ibid.
29 *Fremantle Herald*, 27 September 2009, p. 1.
30 University of Notre Dame, *Politics staff and students support Great 2009 Freo Mayoral Debate*, 15 September 2009, University of Notre Dame, Fremantle, viewed 19 February 2014, <http://www.nd.edu.au/news/media-releases/2009/mayoral_debate.shtml>.
31 Transcript of the Great 2009 Freo Mayoral Debate on 22 September 2009. See Appendix 153 in T. Kerr, 'Representing ecological threats and negotiating green built environment', PhD thesis, Curtin University, 2012.
32 *The West Australian*, 17 October 2009, p. 32.
33 Ibid.
34 Ibid.
35 Ibid.
36 Western Australian Electoral Commission, *2009 Ordinary Election Fremantle Results*, Western Australian Electoral Commission, Perth, viewed 19 February 2014, <http://www.elections.wa.gov.au/elections/local/92E12E4F-DF91-462C-A10F-44901E539F15/results/Fremantle>
37 *Promises Made*, B. Pettitt, Fremantle, viewed 19 February 2014 <http://bradpettitt.org/promisesmade.html>.

GREEN CAPITAL

Courtesy of *Fremantle Herald*, 4 July 2009, page 27

Monday's high winds ripped North Port Quay's billboard from its moorings along the Phillimore Street tracks, bent it in half and tossed it onto the footpath.

"Shows what the wind thinks of NPQ," a local inspecting the damage quipped.

"They can't even make a sustainable sign," another observed. There were no injuries or other damage.[1]

Fremantle Herald

On the grey, wet streets of Fremantle it was uncanny seeing the North Port Quay future in tattered ruins. The left half of North Port Quay's billboard by the train line had been torn to the ground, overwhelming the words 'Fremantle – the perfect place for North Port Quay'. Only the lone surfer was left standing on Port Beach, in front of the sea and port facilities, between the words, 'future' and 'It just makes sense'. This sign of nature's violent rejection of the North Port Quay future was not lost on Fremantle audiences. A block away, the *Fremantle Herald* published a close-up of this smashed billboard in a compilation of images of damage in the storm of winter 2009.[2] The newspaper suggested that experienced locals knew nature would overcome North Port Quay, and that its creators were incapable of making anything sustainable. The page also showed extensive beach erosion and storm damage around the construction site of Stockland's Islands of 'environmental sustainability'[3] – apartment blocks on the South Beach dunes. The page headings 'Wave power' and 'Wind power'[4] seemed to parody the ecological-modernisation claims made by Professor Newman, whose office was just a block away from the enigmatic billboard. Just a week before its destruction, Newman argued that Deputy Mayor Dowson should not dismiss North Port Quay for being 'unsustainable' when it was 'much less car-based than urban fringe development'.[5] Newman maintained the project demonstrated 'the next generation of carbon-free technologies in city building'. Nobody at events outside Fremantle had objected to North Port Quay being presented as an example of sustainability, said Newman. 'I have spoken about urban resilience and sustainability, with NPQ as an example, in the US, across Australia and last week in Canada at a big local government sustainability conference', he wrote to the press. 'No-one has said this is obviously "unsustainable", they just want to know more'.[6] Newman made his long conference presentation available to the public on CUSP's website.[7] Slide 139 of Newman's 151-slide presentation featured an aerial rendering of North Port Quay and the words: 'Carbon-free development based on renewables, Smart Grid and electric vehicles'.[8] The presentation contained images of projects from around the world that had appeared earlier in a North Port Quay advertisement.[9] Before the storm, Newman repeatedly defended North Port Quay in public. Against mounting criticism, he insisted that the project's technologies were endorsed by the US Administration: 'Obama is putting billions into smart grids, renewables and electric vehicles – the three components we identified as the basis of NPQ,' he said.[10] 'Al Gore is calling this combination the "Moon Shot" as it will enable us to go 100 per cent renewable in 10 years.' He promised that Curtin University Sustainability Policy Unit would apply its researchers and grant resources towards working on such a combination of technologies at every opportunity. The North Port Quay consortium just happened to be the first 'group of developers willing to try these new ideas'.[11] This would be Newman's last public appeal for local support for the project. Once North Port Quay's billboard came down in the storm, no more was heard from Newman on the project. It was time to forget North Port Quay: the sign had been emptied of everything supporting green meaning. It was no longer of any use to the project's proponents; and, without them pushing the project, North Port Quay would soon also be forgotten by its opponents. But not before Adam McHugh of Murdoch University had taken Professor Newman to task in the press for continuing to spruik North Port Quay's 'supposed "carbon-free" qualities' despite the Australian Competition and Consumer Commission investigation.[12] McHugh targeted Newman for ignoring established methods of carbon accounting.

'[There] are in fact methods to account for carbon, some of which are already enshrined in federal law,' wrote McHugh. 'Perhaps Peter Newman's denial of the existence of these methods is in the past. Perhaps he has developed competency in this area. If so,' McHugh asked, 'could any estimation of NPQ's future net emissions by him or his institute...ever be unbiased?'[13] After the storm, Newman responded to McHugh in a letter to the *Herald* which did not mention North Port Quay.[14] A fatigued Newman, recovering from surgery, concentrated his argument on defending his experimental approach to sustainable built environments. He invited Fremantle community to support such demonstrations of dealing with messy, complicated issues around sustainability.

As a demonstration, North Port Quay showed that the contingent meaning of 'green building' is determined by the ways in which people sense and discuss environmental problems. The politics of green building is, therefore, waged in struggles over the meanings of environmental problems. But playing politics in this field of meaning is complicated by there being no universal perception of environmental problems. The meanings of environmental problems depend on where people stand and what they have experienced. Although the consortium advertised that North Port Quay 'can lead the world in sustainable development'[15] people near the construction site did not see it that way. Simulations of North Port Quay's great seawall reminded them of the threat of rising sea levels without offering them any protection from this inundation. People in Fremantle saw themselves remaining outside the walls having to endure the problem of rising sea levels aggravated by pollution emitted in the construction of North Port Quay's wall, reclaimed land, streets and buildings. To mean 'green building', the project had to deal with the public perception of its environmental threats. But the consortium failed to offer solutions to these environmental threats. The consortium did not seem to take seriously enough the threats inscribed in its project's imagery. North Port Quay did not signify green built environment to many citizens in Fremantle because it offered no solutions to the immediate environmental threats that the project suggested to them. Renderings of the project made the seawall, rising sea levels, construction emissions and beach damage loom large in the minds of local readers. Arguments that the project would mitigate the global threat of climate change were ineffective because even this threat was thought of, by locals, as an immediate threat to the cherished local environment. Sensed as an immediate threat to local environment, climate change was much more moving than if it had been viewed dispassionately – the view offered by proponents – as a scientifically demonstrable phenomenon threatening the whole world a few years from now. Spatially and temporally immediate threats were more meaningful and moti-vating in Fremantle community than the distant future threats suggested by North Port Quay's proponents. This motivational power was derived from a beach, building, streetscape and things such as plants and people in these places being sensed directly and intimately, unlike the more abstract and mediated idea of global environment. People responded conservatively when they saw their sensual relation to things under threat. Community resistance to the project was successful because the dominant environmental problem associated with the project shifted rapidly in public conversation from proponents' description of long-term global ecological threats to opponents' talk of the project immedi-ately threatening their local environment, where beach aesthetics were a powerful trigger for social action. People were moved by an immediate call to the beach, not by a scientific demand for them to make way for a 'significant demonstration of the carbon-constrained future'.[16] Standing for 'our beaches' was a powerful symbol that unified popular resentment against coastal property development. It worked because it engaged people's desire to restore sensual experience of the local environment. This desire for restoration – symbolised in the defence of 'our beaches' – was sufficiently moving and ambiguous for it to be the empty signifier[17] that unified a local popular movement against North Port Quay. This popular movement arose from a shared deeply conservative response to the radical imposition of the consortium's proposed green space for capital accumulation. Although this movement seemed to be progressive in supporting local environ-ment and the electoral successes of a party to the left of Labor, it was driven by a conservative response to radical spatial change. This popular reaction was appropriated successfully by seemingly radical politicians standing for the conservation of beloved places against the threat of radical change driven by emerging technolo-gies of capital accumulation. North Port Quay's proponents were, in fact, the spatial radicals.

North Port Quay can be seen as a demonstration of glo-balised free-market utopianism colliding with a localised spatial utopianism. Representatives of the North Port Quay consortium declared they would mobilise billions of dollars to develop the project as a radically different built environment: a sustainable-development model for urban, carbon-constrained coastal living that would be a new space through which capital would continue to accumulate. Perhaps Greg Poland and his fellow investors chose the seabed site off Port Beach for the same reason that, centuries earlier, Thomas More had thought of carving the island of Utopia off a mainland coast.[18] Society could be reformed, towards the developer's ideal, in a constructed space where people had already been disconnected from existing places, or so More suggested.

Such is the colonial ideal of Australia: discovering, settling and civilising the 'empty' island.

North Port Quay's proponents, and their opponents, also argued that the 345-hectare site at sea could be acquired more cheaply and easily than an equivalent site on nearby land already containing people's homes, stories and institutions. The offshore development site for North Port Quay would produce higher returns on investment because higher prices were paid for coastal than in-land properties within commuter distance of Perth's central business district. But the consortium failed to anticipate the cost of attempting to overcome the local people's deep desire to again experience their cherished time at the beach and the entanglement of these experiences within our insular imagining of Australia.[19] This desire and its entanglements destabilised attempts to represent North Port Quay as a solution to environmental problems. Threats to the realisation of identities, formed around this desire, antagonised locals and unified a popular movement against the project. This movement carried many Greens candidates into elected office and reinforced the ideal of Fremantle being a special place.

Resolution of the North Port Quay issue demonstrated how antagonisms, arising from threatened place relations, can be dealt with through an engaging local public sphere and locally legitimate democratic institutions. However, these local public spheres and democratic institutions are under pressure to reform. Since North Port Quay was rejected by Fremantle Council in late 2009, the Western Australian Government has taken steps to shift authority for urban planning decisions away from local councils to its new regional Development Assessment Panels (DAPs). Barnett's state government claims that these panels have the expertise for dispassionately dealing with property-development projects as well as any environmental issues surrounding them. According to the government, these DAPs will 'improve the planning system by providing more transparency, consistency and reliability in decision making on complex development applications'.[20] Each panel will include three appointed experts 'to strike an appropriate balance between local representation and professional advice in decision making'.[21] This shift in authority for urban-planning decision making from elected local councils towards regional boards, presided by appointed experts, seems to be occurring across Australia:

> The introduction of DAPs is one of the fundamental principles of the national Development Assessment Forum's ('DAF') leading practice model for development assessment...South Australia and New South Wales have already introduced development assessment panels into their planning systems in accordance with the DAF model. Victoria has also recently passed legislation to implement development assessment commissions to perform the role of development assessment panels.[22]

Also, councils in the Perth metropolitan area are being dissolved, replaced by state-appointed commissioners, and merged into larger municipal entities.[23] Generally, senior government officials seem determined to shift institutional handling of antagonisms around property-development proposals away from the people closest to proposed construction sites towards broader geographical institutional politics and industry expertise that favours well-resourced organisations, such as large property developers. Perhaps North Port Quay would have been approved for development by an expert regional panel, as endorsed by its sustainability consultant, Professor Newman. However, it is also likely that the localised antagonism generated in response to the North Port Quay proposal would not have been resolved through the authority of a regional-assessment panel if its decision-making process lacked democratic legitimacy within the local public sphere. If this legitimacy, integral to the hegemonic governance of Australia, is missing, then alternative methods for making people recognise authority may take its place. It has been argued that there are, broadly, two methods of facilitating governance of contemporary society: the generally preferred method being the legitimacy of democratic institutions responding to engaged publics and the secondary method being state coercion of citizens.[24] The case of North Port Quay at the river mouth is a demonstration of the preferred method, but more recently, further upstream, the secondary method has been deployed to suppress important public discussion of Aboriginal affairs at Matagarup, Heirisson Island. Many Aboriginal citizens realise that state violence remains an applied governance method for dealing with their legitimate concerns about place relations on the river.[25] Yet, violence is an unethical method for governing place relations because such relations are never truly fixed or governable. On close examination, place relations are renegotiated continually through expression of people's environmental knowledge, reinforced through sensory experience. What had appeared static is actually moving. In all this complexity and contingency, people are not fully conscious of their own place relations let alone someone else's. The North Port Quay case demonstrates that local citizens may respond to a radical green built environment proposal in a way unforeseen and barely understood by the project's proponents. People's desire to protect and restore the beloved objects in their environment has the potential to contingently unite people in a localised popular movement until the threat has been resolved or a compromise achieved. Given the dominance of capital relations in our globalised contemporary society, it is reasonable to assume that more radical green built environments will be envisaged by small-yet-powerful groups of people for imposition in urban areas around the world in the name of helping to solve global or regional ecological threats. This book suggests that the localised antagonisms and popular social movements – stimulated in response to these impositions – can and should be handled through locally legitimate democratic institutional processes because of the open meaning of ecological threats and the agency of people's affective investments in objects of their local environments. There is a risk that a more regional-ised institutional handling of localised antagonisms may lack local democratic legitimacy, leaving little opportunity for non-violent technologies to deal with antagonisms produced in response to proposed new green zones of capital accumulation.

Notes

1   *Fremantle Herald*, 4 July 2009, p. 27.
2   Ibid.
3   *About Islands*, Stockland Corporation, Sydney, viewed 5 December 2011, <http://www.stockland.com.au/apartments/wa/islands.htm>.
4   *Fremantle Herald*, 4 July 2009, p. 27.
5   *Fremantle Herald*, 27 June 2009, p. 6.
6   Ibid.
7   P. Newman, *Resilient cities: Responding to the crash, peak oil and climate change*, Curtin University Sustainability Policy Institute, Fremantle, viewed 21 October 2009, <http://sustainability.curtin.edu.au/local/docs/Resilent_cities.pdf>.
8   Ibid., p. 139.
9   *Fremantle Gazette*, 10 February 2009, pp. 24–5.
10 *Fremantle Herald*, 27 June 2009, p. 6.
11 Ibid.
12 *Fremantle Herald*, 11 July 2009, p. 5.
13 Ibid.

14 *Fremantle Herald*, 25 July 2009, p. 6.

15 *Fremantle Gazette*, 10 February 2009, pp. 24–5.

16   *Fremantle Herald*, 16 August 2008, pp. 6–7.

17 Laclau, *On Populist Reason*, pp. 104–20.

18 T. More, 'Utopia' in S. Bruce (ed), *Three Early Modern Utopias: Thomas More: Utopia / Francis Bacon: New Atlantis / Henry Neville: The Isle of Pines*, Oxford University Press, Oxford, 1999, pp. 1–148.

19 S. Perera, *Australia and the Insular Imagination: Beaches, Borders, Boats, and Bodies*, Palgrave Macmillan, New York, 2009.

20 *Development Assessment Panel – Questions and Answers*, Government of Western Australia, Perth, 2011, viewed 25 March 2014, <http://daps. planning.wa.gov.au/data/Questions%20and%20Answers/DAP%20 FAQs%20September%202011.pdf>.

21 Ibid., p. 1

22 Ibid.

23 Department of Local Government and Communities, *Metropolitan Reform*, Government of Western Australia, Perth, 2014, viewed 25 March 2014, <http://metroreform.dlg.wa.gov.au/Page. aspx?PID=MetropolitanReform>.

24 See P. Dahlgren, *Media and Political Engagement: Citizens, Communication, and Democracy*, Cambridge University Press, New York, 2009, p. 59. Also S. Hall, C. Critcher, T. Jefferson, J. Clarke & B. Roberts, *Policing the Crisis: Mugging, the State, and Law and Order*, Macmillan, London, 1978, p. 319.

25 T. Kerr & S. Cox, *Setting up the Nyoongar Tent Embassy: a Report on Perth Media*, Ctrl-Z Press, Perth, 2013.

PLACE IN DEMOCRACY

Photograph by Prapti Widinugraheni

'...They paved paradise and put up a parking lot...'[1]

Joni Mitchell

The Cafe Rous roadhouse is surprisingly inviting for a concrete block. It stands alone within an expanse of freshly laid asphalt before a 60-bay truck park that looks like a deserted drive-in movie complex. It is the first building on 27 hectares of land reclaimed[2] in the southeast corner of the seabed site that was sought by the North Port Quay consortium. In 2014, nobody seemed to complain about this new roadhouse service station, which boasts a convenience store, shower facilities, free wi-fi, 'a massage chair and a pin ball machine'. It also offers 'work wear, fishing gear, bait and automotive items and lubes'.[3] This may be paradise for a weary truck driver, dock worker or anyone with the opportunity to enjoy the roadhouse and parking lots scattered all along Rous Head. That this paving over of the sea, by the sea, could be paradise speaks for the complexity of people's place relations. It explains why the ambiguity in Joni Mitchell's 1970 song, 'Big Yellow Taxi', has worked for so many listeners, particularly in Australia. Her lyrics, 'They paved paradise and put up a parking lot', can be so easily sung 'Create paradise and put up a parking lot'.[4] This song that starts out as a complaint against the destruction and commoditisation of nature, turns on the words 'But leave me the birds and the bees, Please!' to become a complaint about relationship loss:

> Late last night
> I heard the screen door slam
> And a big yellow taxi
> Took away my old man[5]

Such ambiguity around human–nature relations has been worked up in subsequent versions of Mitchell's song, including the more intimate ending in Counting Crows' cover featuring Vanessa Carlton:

> *Adam Duritz and Vanessa Carlton:*
> I don't wanna give it
> Why you wanna give it
> Why you wanna giving it all away?
> Hey, hey, hey
> Now you wanna give it

I should wanna give it
Cos you giving it all away…
Vanessa:
Why do you want me?
Why do you want me?
Adam:
Cos you're givin it all away[6]

It no longer matters that in the next and final line, Duritz sings: 'Hey, paved paradise to put up a parking lot'. In the Counting Crows' video clip, fond memories are shown in paved high-density areas while the band plays along in an old deserted theme park and on a boardwalk by the sea. Romance is signified in the messy, colourful, high-density and industrial parts of the city. Background litter, redundant warning signs and graffiti blend with weeds, trees, and high-density neighbourhoods in signifying intimate urban pleasure. The song is not about protecting pristine nature, it is a call to respect people's desire to protect place relations that have been sensed uniquely and intimately through experiences with what is commonly called culture and nature. The clip suggests that we cherish experiences in urban environments, no matter how anthropogenic they may seem. For these environments offer us our memories, and our identities.

Before passing its motion to reject North Port Quay, Fremantle Council supported the city's planning-committee report acknowledging that land reclamation had occurred at Rous Head as recently as 1989, and that more seabed at the proposed North Port Quay site would soon be reclaimed by Fremantle Ports.[7] The volume of reclamation and associated environmental damage for the port's Inner Harbour Deepening Project was deemed acceptable by the planning committee because it was 'much smaller' than the volume and damage proposed by the North Port Quay consortium.[8] The material dredged from the Inner Harbour was deposited 'behind a new seawall directly adjacent to Rous Head', creating the 27 additional hectares of reclaimed land upon which the Cafe Rous service station now stands. The environmental assessment for Fremantle Ports' project identified 'potential impacts of the works upon marine habitats, fauna and water and sediment quality'.[9] When Fremantle Ports dredged the river mouth in 2010 a foul-smelling toxic plume was released that could be sensed not just upstream in the Derbal Yaragan but all the way up to Djarlgarra, the Canning River wetlands in Riverton. The member for Fremantle, Adele Carles, called for the reclamation project to be delayed pending an environmental investigation,[10] but the project went ahead regardless. No popular movement came together to stand in the way of Fremantle Ports' harbour deepening project despite its noticeable alteration of the river, fouling up of local beaches and reclamation of seabed off Rous Head. The absence of a popular movement against this project can be attributed to many factors including the dredging project being represented, generally, in the local public sphere as a preferable option to North Port Quay. Secondly, a rallying cry to 'fight them on the beaches'[11] has more resonance in contemporary Australian culture than a call – had it been worded this way – to 'delay them at the river mouth'. Also, no clear division was produced in public discussion between 'them' and 'us' regarding the harbour deepening project. The working-port town identity was so firmly embedded in local cultural production, that it was self-defeating for local activists to distinguish themselves against a state authority that could so easily position itself with the Dockers and the dockworkers. Finally, any response to stand against the harbour deepening project was undermined by people's prior investments in the state through engagement with its democratic institutions and community identity. This subjectivity to government generally extends to state corporations such as Fremantle Ports.

Understanding and working with subjectivities to institutions and environmental objects should be the first step in designing an appropriate green built environment. For property developers and their consultants, this means resisting the tendency to dismiss the legitimacy of antagonisms produced by the public announcement of their projects. Instead they should be hospitable to the concerns of local citizens, recognising that their environmental relations are threatened and then negotiating these concerns as part of the project design and financial modelling process. Refusing to offer such hospitality in the name of addressing some global future ecological threat does not work because it produces local resistance and marginalises possible contributions by local citizens with expert knowledge and love of their environments. Rejecting localised environmental concerns is, therefore, a significant constraint in addressing ecological crisis. Reducing the complexity of environmental problems to scientifically solvable universal phenomenon, such as climate change, is a political act that supports broad geographies of institutional governance while undermining localised institutional handling of environmental concerns. Seeking a way out of environmental crisis by sterilising environmental relations, or purifying the aesthetics of environmental problems, is a huge mistake. This has become evident by the failure of international forums to produce locally implementable policy for tackling climate change. Shifting environmental damage and pollution out of sight and out of mind remains an important technique of industrialisation. Yet, in a world of 7 billion people, anthropogenic environmental damage is likely to be sensed in some way by people closest to sites of damage. Being hospitable to local people's concerns is probably the most effective way to tackle environmental problems. Those closest to potential sites of environmental damage have the most to lose and are, therefore, most likely to act. They understand environmental problems in their own way but their collective action on localised environmental problems could add up to a radical solution in the age of global environmental crisis.

On the other hand, the road to reducing a multitude of complex environmental challenges to the universal ecological threat of climate change is a political one. Climate change *is a convenient truth* that supports the interests of global organisations and institutions of global governance. But it can also be read in a variety of ways that support local environmental movements. The case of North Port Quay demonstrates that applying a politics of reductive climate-change representation is likely to generate fierce resistance. The act of representing such a reduced version of environmental problems around a building site produces its own resistance in the form of antagonised local citizens who fear losing sensual experiences of cherished environmental objects. So, anyone interested in tackling environmental problems at a particular site must remain hospitable to the knowledge, interests and affective investments of people emotionally invested in the site. Ignoring the powerful agency of threats to their cherished environments through reductionist representation of an ecological threat is likely to constrain the environmental project. Whereas remaining open to and negotiating the multitude of meanings of environmental problems around the site is much more likely to solicit localised support for the project. The organisation behind a green-building proposal should be hospitable to other ways of knowing environmental problems. And so, recognising local concerns should be continued in the age of ecological crisis.

Notes

1   J. Mitchell, 'Big Yellow Taxi', 1970, Joni Mitchell, viewed 17 March 2014, <http://jonimitchell.com/music/song.cfm?id=208>.

2   *Progress on Rous Head development,* 13 June 2013, Fremantle Ports, Fremantle, viewed 27 March 2015, <http://www.fremantleports.com.au/ News/News/Pages/News-Item.aspx?item=213&returnurl=http://www. fremantleports.com.au/News/Newsletters/Pages/Port-News-2013.aspx>

3   *Café Rous,* True Local, Sydney, viewed 17 March 2014, <http://www. truelocal.com.au/business/cafe-rous/north-fremantle>.

4   Mitchell, 'Big Yellow Taxi'.

5   Ibid.

6   T. Mckenzie, J. Mitchell & M. Williams, *Counting Crows Lyrics:* 'Big Yellow Taxi', A-Z Lyrics, viewed 17 March 2014, <http://www.azlyrics.com/ lyrics/countingcrows/bigyellowtaxi.html>.

7   City of Fremantle, *City of Fremantle, Agenda – Ordinary Meeting of Council: 23 September 2009.*

8   Ibid., p. 71.

9   Ibid.

10 A. Carles, *Carles Calls for Deferral of Fremantle Dredging,* Adele Carles, Fremantle, 2010, viewed 25 March 2014, < http://adelecarles.wordpress. com/2010/01/07/carles-calls-for-deferral-of-fremantle-dredging/>.

11 *Fremantle Herald,* 30 August 2008, p. 17.

BIBLIOGRAPHY

Books, journals, minutes and reports

Anderson, B., *Imagined Communities: Reflections on the Origin and Spread of Nationalism*, Verso, London, 1991.

Bakhtin, M. M., *The Dialogic Imagination: Four Essays*, C. Emerson & M. Holquist (trans), University of Texas Press, Austin, 1981.

Balai, L., *Het Slavenschip Leusden: Slavenschepen en de West Indische Compagnie*, 1720-1738, Walberg Pers, Zutphen, 2011.

Bennett, T., *Birth of the Museum: History, Theory, Politics*, Routledge, London, 1995.

Boym, S., 'Nostalgia and its discontents', *The hedgehog Review*, Summer, 2007, pp. 7-18.

Brown, P. M., *The Merchant Princes of Fremantle: The Rise and Decline of a Colonial Elite 1870-1900*, University of Western Australia Press, Nedlands, 1996.

Bunbury, B., *Caught in Time: Talking Australian History.* Fremantle Arts Centre Press, Fremantle, 2006.

Cahill, D. 'New-class discourse and construction of left-wing elites', in M. Sawer & B. Hindness (eds), *Us and Them: Anti-elitism in Australia*, API Network, Australia Research Institute, Perth, 2004, pp. 86-94.

Carter, B. & Nutter, L., *Nyungah Land: Records of Invasion and Theft of Aboriginal Land on the Swan River 1829 – 1850*, Swan Valley Nyungah Community, Guildford, 2005.

Chouliaraki, L., ' Mediation, text and action', in V. K. Bhatia, J. Flowerdew & R. H. Jones (eds), *Advances in Discourse Studies,* Routledge, London, 2008, pp. 211-27.

City of Fremantle, *Agenda – Ordinary Meeting of Council: 23 September 2009*, City of Fremantle, Fremantle, 2009.

City of Fremantle, *Minutes – Ordinary Meeting of Council: 23 September 2009*, City of Fremantle, Fremantle, 2009.

Copjec, J., *Imagine there's no Woman: Ethics and Sublimation*, MIT Press, Cambridge, Massachusetts, 2004.

Corruption and Crime Commission, *Report on the Investigation of Alleged Misconduct Concerning Mr Stephen Lee, Mayor of the City of Cockburn*, Government of Western Australia, Perth, 2008.

Curl, J. S., *The Art and Architecture of Freemasonry: An Introductory Study*, Batsford, London, 1991.

Dahlgren, P., *Media and Political Engagement: Citizens, Communication, and Democracy*, Cambridge University Press, New York, 2009.

Davidson, R. & Davidson, D., *Fighting for Fremantle: the Fremantle Society Story*, Fremantle Society, Fremantle, 2010.

Dryzek, J. S., *The Politics of the Earth: Environmental Discourses*, Oxford University Press, Oxford, 2005.

Ericson, R. V., Baranek, P. M. & Chan, J. B. L., *Negotiating Control: A Study of News Sources*, Open University Press, Milton Keynes, 1989.

Ewers, J. K., *The Western Gateway: A History of Fremantle*, University of Western Australia Press, Nedlands, 1971.

Fiske, J. Hodge, B. & Turner, G., *Myths of Oz: Reading Australian Popular Culture*, Allen & Unwin, North Sydney, 1987.

Gelder, K. & Jacobs, J., *Uncanny Australia: Sacredness and Identity in a Postcolonial Nation*, Melbourne University Press, Carlton South, 1998.

Gore, A., *An Inconvenient Truth*, Paramount Home Entertainment, Australia, 2006.

Haimes, G. A., 'Organizational culture and identity: A case study from the Australian Football League', PhD thesis, Victoria University, Melbourne, 2006.

Hajer, M. A., *The Politics of Environmental Discourse: Ecological Modernization and the Policy Process*, Oxford University Press, Oxford, 1995.

Hall, S., Critcher, C., Jefferson, T., Clarke, J. & Roberts, B., *Policing the Crisis: Mugging, the State, and Law and Order*, Macmillan, London, 1978.

Hartley, J., 'A State of Excitement: Western Australia and the America's Cup', *Cultural Studies*, vol. 2, no. 1, 1988, pp. 117-26.

Hartley, J., 'Expatriation: Useful astonishment as cultural studies', *Cultural Studies*, vol. 6, no. 3, 1992, p. 449-67.

Harvey, D., *Justice, Nature, and the Geography of Difference*, Blackwell Publishers, Cambridge, Massachusetts, 1996.

Harvey, D., *Spaces of Hope*, Edinburgh University Press, Edinburgh, 2000.

Howard, E., *Garden Cities of To-morrow*, Faber and Faber, London, 1946.

Hudson-Rodd, N. & Farrell, G. A., 'The Round House Gaol: Western Australia's first lunatic asylum', *Australia and New Zealand Journal of Mental*

Health Nursing, vol. 7, no. 4, 1998, pp. 152-62.

Hughes, J. D., 'Early Greek and Roman environmentalists', in L. J. Bilsky (ed), *Historical Ecology: Essays on Environment and Social Change*, Kennikat Press, Port Washington, 1980, pp. 45-59.

Hutchison, D., *Fremantle Walks*, Fremantle Arts Centre Press, Fremantle, 2006.

Kaufman, E. N., 'Architectural representation in Victorian England', *Journal of the Society of Architectural Historians*, vo. 46, no. 1, 1987, pp. 30-38.

Kelsall Binet Architects, *Monument Hill Memorial Reserve Fremantle Conservation Plan*, City of Fremantle, Fremantle, 2009.

Kenworthy, J. R., 'The eco-city: ten key transport and planning dimensions for sustainable city development', *Environment and Urbanization*, vol. 18, no. 1, 2006, 67-85.

Kerr, T., 'Sustainability discourse and the green building', Honours thesis, Curtin University, 2008.

Kerr, T., 'Representing ecological threats and negotiating green built environments', PhD thesis, Curtin University, 2012.

Kerr, T., 'Reproducing temples in Fremantle', *International Journal of Heritage Studies*, vol. 18, no. 1, 2012, pp. 1-17.

Kerr, T. & Cox, S., *Setting up the Nyoongar Tent Embassy: a Report on Perth Media*, Ctrl-Z Press, Perth, 2013.

Koeppel, S. & Ürge-Vorsatz, D., *Assessment of Policy Instruments for Reducing Greenhouse Gas Emissions from Buildings*, United Nations Environment Programme and Central European University, Budapest, 2007.

Laclau, E., *On Populist Reason*, Verso, London, 2005.

Madew, R., *Directors' Report*, Green Building Council Australia, Sydney, 2008.

Malthus, R. T., 'An essay on the Principle of Population: The Sixth Edition (1826) with Variant Readings from the Second Edition (1803)', in E. A. Wrigley & D. Souden (eds), *The Works of Thomas Robert Malthus*. William Pickering, London, 1986.

Meadows, D. H., Meadows, D. L., Randers, J. & Behrens III, W. W., *The Limits to Growth: a Report for the Club of Rome's Project on the Predicament of Mankind*, Universe Books, New York, 1972.

Mickler, S., 'Curators and the colony: Managing the past at Rottnest Island Museum', *Continuum: The Australian Journal of Media & Culture*, vol. 3, no. 1, 1990, pp. 84-100.

Mickler, S., 'The battle for Goonininup', *Arena*, vol. 96, Spring, 1991, pp. 69-88.

Miller, J., *Tackling Global Climate Change: Meeting Local Priorities*, World Green Building Council, Toronto, 2010.

More, T., 'Utopia' in S. Bruce (ed), *Three Early Modern Utopias: Thomas More:*

Utopia / Francis Bacon: New Atlantis / Henry Neville: The Isle of Pines, Oxford University Press, Oxford, 1999, pp. 1-148.

Nadler, S., *Spinoza's Ethics: An Introduction*, Cambridge University Press, Cambridge, 2006.

Nowland, G. 'Fremantle: The port as a threshold of consciousness in the novel', *Westerly: a Quarterly Review*, no. 51, 2006, pp. 145-58.

Perera, S., *Australia and the Insular Imagination: Beaches, Borders, Boats, and Bodies*, Palgrave Macmillan, New York, 2009.

Porter, R., Moorhouse, J., Kins, A. & Peddie, B., *Our Place: Cultural Policy and Plan*, City of Fremantle, Fremantle, 1999, p. 12.

Rich, P. J., *Elixir of Empire: The English Public Schools, Ritualism, Freemasonry, and Imperialism*, Regency Press, London, 1989.

Rogers, P. P., Jalal, K. F. & Boyd, J. A., *An Introduction to Sustainable Development*, Earthscan, London, 2008.

Rowling, J. K., *Harry Potter and the Philosopher's Stone*, Bloomsbury, London, 1997.

Sachs, W., 'In the wake of Rio', in W. Sachs (ed), *Global Ecology: A New Arena of Political Conflict*, Fernwood Publishing, Halifax, 1993, pp. 3-21.

Schneider, S. H., Semenov, S., Patwardhan, A., Burton, I., Magadza, C. H. D., Oppenheimer, M., et al. 'Assessing key vulnerabilities and the risk from climate change', in M. L. Parry, O. F. Canziani, J. P. Palutikof, P. J. van der Linden & C. E. Hanson (eds), *Climate Change 2007: Impacts, Adaptation and Vulnerability*. Cambridge University Press, Cambridge, 2007, pp. 779-810.

Scollon, R. & Scollon, S. W., *Discourses in Place: Language in the Material World*, Routledge, London, 2003.

Shorto, R., *Amsterdam: A History of the World's Most Liberal City*, Little, Brown, London, 2014.

Statham-Drew, P., *James Stirling: Admiral and Founding Governor of Western Australia*, University of Western Australia Press, Crawley, 2003.

Stratton, J., 'Dying to come to Australia: Asylum seekers, tourists and death', in R. Summo-O'Connell (ed), *Imagined Australia: Reflections around the Reciprocal Construction of Identity between Australia and Europe*, Peter Lang, Bern, 2009, pp. 57-87.

Tull, M. *A Community Enterprise: The History of the Port of Fremantle, 1897 to 1997*, International Maritime Economic History Association, St. John's, 1997.

Walker, C., *Highway to Hell: The Life and Death of AC/DC Legend Bon Scott*, Verse Chorus Press, Portland, 2007.

While, A., Jonas, A. E. G. & Gibbs, D., 'From sustainable development to carbon control: eco-state restructuring and the politics of urban and regional development', *Transactions of the Institute of British Geographers*, vol. 35, no. 1, 2010, pp. 76-93.

White, J. 'Henry Reveley, architect and engineer', *Journal of the Royal Western Australia Historical Society*, vol. 7, no. 8, 1976, pp. 24-42.

World Commission on Environment and Development, *Our Common Future*, Oxford University Press, Oxford, 1987.

Young, S., 'The origins and evolving nature of ecological modernization', in S. Young (ed), *The Emergence of Ecological Modernization: Integrating the Environment and the Economy?*, Routledge, London, 2000, pp. 1-40.

Newspapers and television

ABC News WA
The Australian Financial Review
The Australian
Fremantle Herald
Fremantle Gazette
Sydney Morning Herald
The West Australian

Websites

abc.net.au
abs.gov.au
acdc.com
adelecarles.wordpress.com
ap.org
awm.gov.au
azlyrics.com
bca.gov.sg
bradpettitt.org
crikey.com.au
elections.wa.gov.au
flyingangel.org.au
fremantle.wa.gov.au
fremantleports.com.au
freoview.wordpress.com
gbca.org.au
gg.gov.au
google.com
greenleft.org.au

haldenburns.com.au
jonimitchell.com
kingjamesbibleonline.org
nd.edu.au
nobelprize.org
northportquay.com.au
parliament.wa.gov.au
perthnow.com.au
savefreobeaches.com
smh.com.au
southbeachvillage.com.au
stockland.com.au
sustainability.curtin.edu.au
strzeleckigroup.com.au
theaustralian.com.au
truelocal.com.au
wa.gov.au
watoday.com.au
worldgbc.org

INDEX